The Young Adult's Guide to

Robert's Rules of
ORDER

*How to Run Meetings for Your
Club or Organization*

By: Hannah Litwiller

THE YOUNG ADULT'S GUIDE TO ROBERT'S RULES OF ORDER: HOW TO RUN MEETINGS FOR YOUR CLUB OR ORGANIZATION

1405 SW 6th Avenue • Ocala, Florida 34471 • Phone 800-814-1132 • Fax 352-622-1875
Website: www.atlantic-pub.com • Email: sales@atlantic-pub.com
SAN Number: 268-1250

Library of Congress Cataloging-in-Publication Data

Names: Litwiller, Hannah, 1994- | Robert, Henry M. (Henry Martyn), 1837-1923.
  Robert's rules of order.
Title: The young adult's guide to Robert's rules of order : how to run meetings for your club or
  organization / by Hannah Litwiller.
Description: Ocala, Florida : Atlantic Publishing Group, Inc., [2016] | Includes bibliographical
  references, webography and index.
Identifiers: LCCN 2016039289 (print) | LCCN 2016044734 (ebook) | ISBN 9781620231715
  (alk. paper) | ISBN 1620231719 (alk. paper) | ISBN 9781620231722 (ebook)
Subjects: LCSH: Parliamentary practice.
Classification: LCC JF515 .L66 2016 (print) | LCC JF515 (ebook) | DDC 060.4/2—dc23
LC record available at https://lccn.loc.gov/2016039289

Printed in the United States

PROJECT MANAGER AND EDITOR: Rebekah Sack • rsack@atlantic-pub.com
INTERIOR LAYOUT AND JACKET DESIGN: Nicole Sturk • nicolejonessturk@gmail.com
COVER DESIGN: Jackie Miller • millerjackiej@gmail.com

Reduce. Reuse.
RECYCLE.

A decade ago, Atlantic Publishing signed the Green Press Initiative. These guidelines promote environmentally friendly practices, such as using recycled stock and vegetable-based inks, avoiding waste, choosing energy-efficient resources, and promoting a no-pulping policy. We now use 100-percent recycled stock on all our books. The results: in one year, switching to post-consumer recycled stock saved 24 mature trees, 5,000 gallons of water, the equivalent of the total energy used for one home in a year, and the equivalent of the greenhouse gases from one car driven for a year.

Over the years, we have adopted a number of dogs from rescues and shelters. First there was Bear and after he passed, Ginger and Scout. Now, we have Kira, another rescue. They have brought immense joy and love not just into our lives, but into the lives of all who met them.

We want you to know a portion of the profits of this book will be donated in Bear, Ginger and Scout's memory to local animal shelters, parks, conservation organizations, and other individuals and nonprofit organizations in need of assistance.

– Douglas & Sherri Brown,
President & Vice-President of Atlantic Publishing

Table of Contents

Foreword: Robert's Rules of Organizations—Meetings

It thrills me that such an invaluable piece of work such as this exists to guide students in student organizations. So often I have seen student-run groups dissipate as a result of issues, every single one of which has been addressed within this book. Hence the fact that it has been updated to reflect the challenges that arise in organizations with younger generations is ideal. Everything from planning the purpose of meetings, mechanisms of communication, assessing and evaluating how a meeting, and how to be a better listener (a priceless piece of advice far too often ignored) is covered in this book.

At the outset, the book covers determining the purpose of meetings. It's something that sounds so simple but yet is often neglected as a tedious and unnecessary step, if not completely overlooked. The need for a meeting is understood, but the purpose is often muddled, resulting in a meeting that may run for hours and accomplish little to nothing. Thus in chapter 4, the discussion of whether or not a meeting is necessary is also vital to preventing the dreaded eternal three-hour-long meeting.

It makes me smile to see a chapter dedicated to communication so early on in the book. Despite the fact that many young adults and youth would consider themselves quite savvy in the *means* of communication, the *mechanisms* used frequently need refining, which this text lends itself to quite well. Chapter 3 does a fine job of discussing a core selection of applications and platforms for not only planning the meeting but in effect having a virtual meeting as well.

Chapters 4, 5, 6, and 7 provide insight to one of the most vital elements to having a successful meeting. The planning discussed in chapters 4 and 5 is crucial to ensuring that everyone is on the same page. I love that chapter 4 clearly delineates *good* and *bad* things to say in clear, plain language. The explanations provided offer core elements to understanding effective team communication, a lesson that is not generally taught in the context of standard secondary education curricula. Chapter 6 offers a sort of toolbox for readers to draw from to get a meeting started and getting attendees engaged. Though some of these are tried-and-true classics, there is room for creativity built within the text designed to inspire readers.

Chapter 7 guides readers in avoiding the pitfalls of meetings, which can easily occur in the context of a student- and youth-run organization. Determining who is the best individual to run a meeting is an invaluable discussion. I love that there is also a discussion on avoiding one person having too much control. Lastly, the concept of facilitation within a meeting is discussed—a concept I didn't even know (not by name, at least) until grad school! To learn that lesson in a practical context is an extremely viable skill that this text enables readers to learn at a much earlier stage in life.

Chapters 9, 10, and 11 offer a troubleshooting tool kit that offer great tips on how to prepare and present data at a meeting—and why it's important to do so in chapter 9. Chapter 10 outlines how to deal with common problems that arise in the context of meetings (e.g. the inevitable isolated situation which dominates a discussion ... for far more time than the meeting was even scheduled for!). Lastly, chapter 11 offers a wonderful discussion on how to ensure your meeting ends on a high note.

Chapters 8 and 12 offer practical guidance for evaluating and assessing how the meeting went. I would also contend far too many individuals—

youth or otherwise—would miss this vital step as well. How can you improve on your meetings if you don't assess them? Why is evaluating how your meetings went important? These chapters provide insight into those questions.

Student organizations at any stage in life offer invaluable lessons that cannot be taught in any other environment. There is so much to learn, so many memorable experiences to be had in the context of these groups that cannot be replicated in any other venue or set of circumstances. This text provides all the tools youth and young adults need to ensure that those memories are positive ones.

Melanie Norwood,
Treasurer, Graduate Student Council
Doctoral Student, University of Illinois at Chicago

Melanie Norwood is a doctoral student in Criminology, Law and Justice at the University of Illinois at Chicago. She has been involved in numerous student organizations throughout her academic career. She is currently involved in the Graduate Student Council and a member of several committees within the university despite being in the final stages of her degree program. She has been teaching in the university environment for ten years and frequently mentors undergraduate students in the course of her work.

Introduction

When you think about running a meeting for a group, what comes to mind? Do you picture members of the incredibly bored Student Council sitting in a crowded room, looking at their phones and pretending to listen to you? Do you imagine your prom committee arguing over decorations, unable to make decisions, and erupting into fistfights while you helplessly try to maintain order? Or do you see these members participating and engaged, solving problems, and even having fun?

If you shudder at the idea of running a meeting or have nightmares about angry committee members starting a war over decorations, I have some bad news: Meetings happen everywhere, not just at school. While you might not worry about your junior prom after graduating high school, you'll still have to attend meetings throughout your life, no matter what career path you choose.

Hollywood producers have meetings. The White House has meetings. Jane Austen fan clubs have meetings. Even evil secret societies probably hold meetings where they solve problems, sacrifice goats, and talk about ruling the world.

Let's face it—meetings are a fact of life. And that's OK.

Learning how to run a meeting is essential to staying on task and making sure your group accomplishes goals and solves problems. Conflict, miscommunication, and repetition ("We've heard this idea about the 'Die Hard' prom theme a million times!") can all be avoided if you understand how to run a meeting properly.

Luckily, we've got you covered. Throughout the course of this book, you'll learn a few trade secrets or two about holding successful meetings—including initial planning, setting objectives, and even how to make meetings fun and enjoyable. With a little planning and communication, everyone will know what to expect at the meeting: who will attend, where it will be held, and its purpose and goals. Speakers and presenters need to know what to do before, during, and after the meeting, and the better you know the people in attendance, the better you can shape an effective agenda. I'll share a variety of techniques to encourage participation, and, best of all, I'll also introduce your new BFF as a meeting leader—Robert of "Robert's Rules of Order," in quick references throughout. You'll get to know Robert swiftly and easily, without any painful small talk.

This book is written for the meeting leader, but you can also learn a lot even if you're just initially attending the meetings for the free food. You'll be able to set up and conduct meetings, stand out from the crowd, and become valuable to your group. You'll become an effective leader in and out of the meeting room. The skills you'll learn while running a meeting can be translated easily to everyday life and will hopefully be valuable throughout your career as an awesome leader/meeting planner extraordinaire.

Before we go on, it is important to make a quick distinction: meetings that are run according to Robert's Rules are very different from meetings run in the world of "work." Work meetings are run by a boss, while Robert's Rules meetings are designed for a room of equals—a place where no one is in the "boss" of anyone else. The purpose of this book is to mesh the fundamental qualities and traditions of Robert's Rules with meetings that you, as a leader of a group or organization in your school, might be leading (in the 21st century). Please be aware that this book covers all kind of meetings and offers up different kinds of examples—work-type meetings as well as meetings run by Robert's Rules.

So, while some of the traditions from Robert's Rules might sound a little old-school—*Mr. Chairman, I move that the motion be amended by adding the following words . . .* —it's kind of cool to see how meetings began. You'll learn the principals of Robert's Rules, and the meat of this book is going to show you how to translate those fundamental qualities into a modern meeting that you can have among your peers.

But, before we jump right into it, we should pause and really explain who the heck this Robert guy is and what he has to do with meetings.

What is Robert's Rules of Order?

The infamous Robert was a lieutenant colonial in the U.S. Army Corps of Engineers. He was really good at running meetings, so he actually crafted up a small guide that's commonly called a "pocket manual." That was in 1876. Today, the Robert's Rules of Order is as thick and heavy as a dictionary, tallying up to over 800 pages of masterful (and dense!) meeting-running material.

So, what does all of this mean for you? Jurassic Parliament, a company established by Ann Macfarlane and Andrew Estep, explains, "[Robert's Rules] contain some simple guidelines that can transform your meetings. A client recently told us that applying these guidelines had cut an average of 90 minutes from their board meetings" (**www.jurassicparliament.com/ roberts-rules-of-order**).

Saving time and following simple guidelines sounds like a no-brainer, right? The Jurassic Parliament website goes on to break down the fundamental principles of Robert's Rules into three simple takeaways:

1. The person running the meeting is the servant of the group, and the group is the final authority.

2. All members have equal rights, privileges, and obligations. To ensure this, no one may speak a second time until everyone who wishes to do so has spoken once.

3. Courtesy and respect are required at all times.

When you look at it, at its core, the idea of using Robert's Rules is to make sure that everyone is heard. All right. Enough chit-chat. Are you ready to learn how to plan meetings and be an effective leader?

Let's get started.

1

Meeting Basics

S o, what is a meeting, anyway?

While definitions of a meeting may differ, the basic idea is that a meeting is a "collaborative work in progress." It's a gathering of three or more people sharing common objectives where communication (whether spoken or written) is a way to achieve those objectives. And in my eyes, it isn't a true meeting unless someone has brought donuts.

Fast Fact

"Robert's Rules of Order" was first published as a book in February 1876 by then U.S. Army Major Henry Martyn Robert to give guidance and order to meetings (**http://extension .illinois.edu**).

I've created a checklist for those instances when you want to make sure you are indeed attending a meeting. Feel free to copy this page and carry it with you at all times, just in case!

1. Are people are collaborating and working together to solve a problem?

    Yes   **No**

2. Have three or more people gathered together to communicate and share common objectives?

    Yes   **No**

3. Did someone bring donuts?[1]

    Yes   **No**

Remember that a meeting has specific content and a purpose. It determines who should attend, what needs to be discussed, and how information is presented. Other considerations that influence a meeting's success are the date, time, place, and whether people need to be face-to-face or can just talk electronically.

Not all meetings are created equal. There are many different kinds of meetings that we'll discuss later on in Chapter 2, and the type you choose depends on the people, the content, the process, and the purpose of the meeting. The idea of having a common objective will be valuable to you when we discuss the what, who, and when of your meetings in Chapter 4.

---

1. Okay, so this isn't *really* a meeting requirement. But I'm a whole-hearted believer that donuts make everything better.

ROBERT'S RULES QUICK REFERENCE:
How to Handle a Main Motion

* Nothing can happen without a motion on the floor *

What is a main motion?	A main motion is when you want to propose a new idea or action.
How do I get the floor?	Raise your hand when no one else has the floor The chairperson (leader of the discussion) will call you by name
How do I propose my motion?	Once recognized, you will say: **"I move that . . ."** or "**I move to . . .**" Another member will second the motion by saying: **"Second," "I second it,"** or **"I second the motion."** The chair says: **"It is moved and seconded that . . . Are you ready for the question?"**

If you're not used to attending meetings often, it can get confusing when you're trying to determine a good meeting versus a bad one. Know that the basic, overall goal is to make sure people feel like they've accomplished or learned something.

A good meeting is when you get stuff done.

Fast Fact

Robert's Rules is by far the most popular of parliamentary procedure, used by approximately 80 percent of groups (**http://extension.illinois.edu**).

Still confused? I've written two more example checklists that will inform you whether you're running a good meeting or a bad meeting. And good news — donuts are involved.

Good Meetings vs. Bad Meetings

The Scene: You're an aspiring playwright and leader of the drama club. You have just announced your new play "The Hole Story — The Origin of the Donut" to the entire school and are planning to hold auditions the following week. Now, you have to hold a meeting to determine how you'll publicize the auditions.

How do you know if it's a good meeting?

- You can share important information with members of your meeting.

  "I've announced the new play to the entire school! It's a brand-new piece about the creation of the donut and its impact in modern society!"

- There is interaction and discussion with others.

  "I've also heard that people are generally excited about the new play about the origin of donuts! What have you heard?"

- Peers can ask questions, and you can answer them. It gives you the chance to see other perspectives on issues.

  "How do we start publicity for auditions, Hannah?"

  "I plan on handing out donuts to the entire school!"

- Peers are engaged. They're asking questions and are involved in the conversation. You're not talking to an empty, dead room — you're talking a group of people who are interested in your plans and ideas.

  "How do you plan on paying for the donuts? Will you bake your own or buy them from the store?"

- It's a great opportunity to direct peers in joint projects.

  "Let's get into groups and discuss how we'll pay for free donuts for the entire school!"

- Important issues can be discussed with everyone in one location.

"Most people don't think handing out free donuts is a good idea. Drama club needs to think about different methods of publicity."

- You can use the time to teach people how to work through a problem.

    "OK everyone, let's think this through and find a better method."

- Learn about others' experiences, and help everyone learn more from them.

    "During my experience as an employee of the local donut shop, my boss often had me stand outside in a giant donut costume to get customers. We can probably borrow it!"

- The meeting helps your peers work together and feel more like a team or community.

    "That sounds like a great idea. We'll borrow the donut suit to publicize for auditions!"

- The meeting gives you a chance to demonstrate and improve your leadership skills.

    "As director of this meeting, I, Hannah, volunteer to dress up in the donut suit to publicize for 'The Hole Story — The Origin of the Donut!'"

- Someone has brought chocolate donuts to the meeting and is willing to share with others.[2]

    "All hail Hannah! She's brought us food!"

---

2. Or any other variety of donut.

How do you know if it's a bad meeting?

- The meeting is not planned properly, and people feel like they're wasting their time.

  "I could have started my math homework ages ago instead of worrying about donuts!"

- The wrong people are in attendance.

  "This isn't the meeting for the gardening club! Why am I even here? I hate donuts!"

- The right people are not included.

  "Is anyone from Drama Club even here? They're the ones running auditions!"

- There is no real reason for the meeting.

  "Auditions aren't until November, and it's only September 1!"

- The same things could be accomplished through other means.

  "We could have used Google™ forms to plan out the date of auditions instead of arguing about it!"

- People do not show up, they arrive late, or they leave early.

  "I thought the meeting was at four in the morning, not four in the afternoon!"

- Meetings become redundant and cover the same issues repeatedly without reaching a conclusion or accomplishing anything.

> *"We've been talking about the probability of a donut sale for weeks, and no one has volunteered!"*

- Some people doze off, doodle, or have private conversations.

  "Hey, dude, check out my drawing of a radioactive donut! It's way more interesting than this meeting!"

- The meeting goes on too long, does not accomplish everything, and people leave expressing relief that it's finally over.

  "Urgh, I never thought I'd be happy to get back to math tutoring!"

- Meetings are sometimes dominated by one or two people, and others are not encouraged to participate.

  "Hannah and Jesse have been arguing about the donut suit for three hours, and no one has been able to get a word in edgewise! I hate this meeting!"

- People are taking everyone's time talking about unrelated information.

  "Forget about play auditions—guess what? I just ate an entire box of donuts by myself in under four minutes!"

- They launch personal attacks on others.

  "Well, 'The Origin of the Donut' is a stupid play idea anyway!"

- People might become hungry and grumpy due to the fact that there are no donuts in sight, but you've been talking about them for hours.

  "My stomach is beginning to eat itself, and it's all your fault!"

While you probably aren't planning on performing a version of "The Hole Story" anytime soon (although I think it sounds like a great idea), these examples of a good meeting and a bad meeting show how important running a good meeting is. You want to make sure you're listening to other people and that they feel important. You also want to make sure you're accomplishing important tasks and solving problems—otherwise, your peers won't want to attend your meetings anymore. And how will you cast "The Hole Story—The Origin of the Donut" if no one shows up to Drama Club?

Fast Fact ——————————————————

Over 10 billion donuts are made in the U.S. each year (**www .lamars.com**).

2

Different Kinds of Meetings:
Prom Edition

Y ou've decided to hold a meeting, but how will you accomplish your goals and objectives? One trick to holding a great meeting is to figure out the type of meeting you want to have. This can be accomplished through understanding your purpose and the goal of the meeting.

Some meetings require many people, while others are easier with fewer participants. Consider the goals for your meeting and determine which format is better for each of your various meetings.

The goal of most meetings is to give out information or to solve a problem, but there are variations on these purposes. After you determine whether your meeting should dispense information or solve a problem, decide which of the following meetings you need to prepare.

Say you're the chair for your dinosaur-themed prom. You decide to hold a meeting for your ten- member committee. This handy guide will help you decide what kind of meeting to hold and how to work with your peers in order to create an effective meeting.

Problem-Solving Meetings

You've got 99 problems, and they're all about the budget for the decoration committee. You don't have enough money to decorate the dance floor—and there's no way the school will let you make a giant Tyrannosaurus Rex as the centerpiece for prom. So, how are you going to solve this budget crisis? Hold a problem-solving meeting.

A problem-solving meeting can be held when changes need to be made. For these meetings to be successful, two things have to happen: Attendees must understand that there is a problem, and they must agree that changes are needed. If your participants do not agree, they will not be helpful or productive in a meeting. For example, if Joey and Rachel don't think you need a huge mechanical Tyrannosaurus Rex for prom, they won't contribute or help you figure out a new budget plan.

When inviting others to your meeting, remember to choose people who understand that a change is needed and who have the power to make the change happen. These people will need to find ways to convince participants before the meeting that a problem exists and things need to change. For example, choosing someone who is super into dinosaurs and is incredibly enthusiastic about the Tyrannosaurus Rex centerpiece will be more likely to help you make a decision and solve a problem.

Decision-Making Meetings

There are times in any group when decisions need to be made. Sometimes, you have multiple choices ("Should we use dinosaurs from the Jurassic Period or the Mesozoic Period?"), and, sometimes, you need to create the choices and turn them over to a group for a decision ("Let's see if people want to use palm trees or just rocks for the photo booth.") If you are seeking answers, you need to set a problem-solving meeting as explained above.

Decision-making meetings should usually involve fewer than 15 people, but you shouldn't go above 30. Having more people will actually prevent a decision from being made. Choose your attendees carefully, and outline the steps to reach a decision before the meeting begins. There isn't any reason to waste time with details that should be clearly outlined before the meeting.

Fast Fact ─────────────────────────

By far, the most common meeting complaint is when no decision has been made (**http://attentiv.com**).

Decision-making meeting outline

1. Fully explain the problem.

   "We need to figure out when we should have prom!"

2. Discuss it.

   "When would be the best weekend to have prom? Does anyone have any ideas?"

3. Explain what should be accomplished in the meeting.

   "Let's decide when prom should be held by the end of this meeting."

4. Establish criteria to be used to evaluate alternatives.

   "Let's make sure there isn't anything on the calendar that will conflict with our dates for prom."

5. Discuss possible solutions.

   "It looks like we can have the prom April 28 or May 4, but May 4 is also the day of the band concert."

6. Make decisions about the alternatives.

   "Let's choose April 28 for the prom!"

Planning Meetings

One reason for planning meetings is to head off anticipated problems. The same principles apply to a planning meeting as a problem-solving meeting, so you can use much of the information discussed above. There are three types of planning meetings:

- Short-Term Plans

  "Let's figure out when we'll work on the giant fern decorations next week."

- Long-Term Goals

  "How many ferns do we want to make? I suggest over 100."

- Long-Term Problem Solving

  "Where will we store our 100 giant ferns after prom is over?

Short-term planning meetings should require only a few people. Long-term planning may require more people, because there are more duties to be handled.

Fast Fact

The average meeting length is between 30-60 minutes (**http://attentiv.com**).

ROBERT'S RULES QUICK REFERENCE:
How a Motion Will Be Considered

- Members are allowed to debate the motion

- Members must get permission to have the floor from the chair while debating, with one person speaking at a time

- The member responsible for the motion may speak first

- Debate must deal only with the motion being discussed

- Debate ends when two-thirds of the assembly votes for closure or by order of the chair if no one wants to debate further

Meetings for Reporting and Making Presentations

Believe it or not, these kinds of meetings are often misused and overused. While you might think these kinds of meetings would take longer, it's actually more helpful to have quick reports and presentations so people don't get bored.

But, why should you hold these kinds of meetings? Well, if you're in charge of the prom committee, you might want to make sure that certain work on the decorations is being done. That means you can call a reporting meeting to verify what has been accomplished and who is performing the work. The participants report progress to you so you can see what else needs to be done. Doing more is probably a waste of time unless you are searching for problems.

You'll also want to make sure that someone is at the meeting who is able to answer questions and can keep the meeting focused. Another person should be assigned to record all problems and other important details as they are discussed, like a secretary. If you're able to keep the meeting on task and remember to record it properly, these seemingly boring meetings about progress will help you out in the long run—especially if you're trying to figure out how many giant ferns you still need to make for Dinosaur Prom!

Some meetings try to avoid participation during reports and presentations, but people need to be encouraged to ask questions and to share their thoughts. While it may seem scary, question and answer sessions can give you valuable information to add to the report when they are handled properly.

Feedback Meetings

Asking for people's opinions, thoughts, and suggestions can produce valuable information and opportunities for members of your organization to hear others' ideas.

Feedback meetings need to be well-planned and organized. Just like meetings for reports and presentations, you'll need a good leader to oversee participants and keep them involved and focused on the subjects at hand. It's easy for these feedback discussions to get off track. The leader needs to only guide the meeting and keep your peers focused.

If you're the meeting leader, you have to stay calm. When comments are negative, you can't take it personally or be defensive. Remember, you asked for the opinions, and some people won't agree with the information being presented. Unfortunately, not everyone will be crazy about your mechanical Tyrannosaurus Rex centerpiece, or your 100 giant ferns, or even your choice of donuts at the meeting. It's up to you to stay calm and collected in the face of people who might complain and make you upset.

It's important to keep a secretary at these meetings, too. A qualified person should record details of the meeting right away and produce a written record that will settle disputes about what was said.

Meetings That Focus on Multiple Tasks

Some meetings can contain some reporting, a presentation, some problem solving, and decision-making. Whenever a meeting shifts to a different type of procedure, it needs to be handled in an appropriate manner. If you need to talk about decorations, fundrasing, and the after-prom party, you'll want to make sure that you have organized your meeting correctly.

These shifts need to be handled smoothly, or your attendees will be confused and will miss important parts of the meeting. If you're the meeting leader, be prepared to shift from one process to another. I suggest using a donut break to keep people on track, but the shifting process is up to you!

ROBERT'S RULES QUICK REFERENCE:
How to Call for Orders of the Day

Why would I want to do this?

You would do so if the chairperson is not following the agenda discussed at the beginning of the meeting.

- Without the need for being called on, you say, **"Call for orders of the day."**

Nominal Group Meetings

This is a structured meeting where attendees submit their individual ideas in writing, and they are then reported to the group. This process can encourage participation from the largest number of attendees. You can use it when the attendees are familiar with the information and can offer useful ideas. Brainstorming is less productive when people need more information to give their comments.

Say you're trying to figure out what the menu should be for the prom dinner, but many people in your group are shy and are uncomfortable speaking around others. Using a nominal group meeting, where ideas are written down instead of spoken out loud, would ideally encourage quieter members of your meetings to participate.

The nominal group meeting occurs in a process:

1. The facilitator poses a question and asks for suggestions.

   "What should be on the menu for the Dinosaur Prom dinner?"

2. Each person composes suggestions and ideas.

   "I'll give you ten minutes to think of ideas! All suggestions are welcome!"

3. A report of the ideas is created and shared with the group.

   "The most popular ideas are dinosaur chicken nuggets, broccoli, and a chocolate fountain that looks like a volcano."

4. After comments are shared, participants may build on them.

   "I love the idea of dinosaur chicken nuggets, but we'll need a vegetarian option, too. What about tofu nuggets?"

5. These steps can be repeated until you've figured out what you want on the menu.

   "We've finally decided what we want on the menu! Let's have a donut break and celebrate!"

Brainstorming Meetings

You can accomplish a lot with two or more people working together. This is especially true when the right people are on the same team with a strong leader. Remember, the more people you include in a planning meeting or discussion, the stronger the leader needs to be.[3]

Feedback and suggestions from multiple people will let you evaluate positive and negative parts of any situation. When the situation is complex, you'll need to involve more people whose perspectives and ideas can be valuable to you. Choose participants carefully, and include people with different specialties. What are the problems you need to address, and who will provide useful input? Those are the people you need to invite. For example, if you want to brainstorm ideas about the after-prom activities, it might be a good idea to invite someone who has experience planning games and another person who understands the after-prom budget.

You do need practical and analytical people, but don't overlook creative members of your club or organization—you need to develop a plan after the problem is identified. Coming up with the initial idea is only the first step. After you have the idea or a possible solution, the hard work starts. Creative individuals give you the imagination and innovation to make the idea work.

The awesome part about bringing the right people together to brainstorm is that a well-chosen group of smart people is able to achieve a lot when you combine their abilities. Different life experiences and thought processes are valuable when you're trying to come up with ideas—don't underestimate that.

---

3. By the way, I don't mean the kind of strong where you have bulging muscles and can lift over 700 pounds. I mean the kind of strong where you're able to stand your ground and keep things on track. But if you can lift over 700 pounds, people will probably listen to you anyway.

Fast Fact

The most common type of meeting is a staff meeting, or a meeting for the entire organization (**http://attentiv.com/america-meets-a-lot**).

Brainstorming steps

1. The leader lists all ideas on a display board.

   "So, we've got a giant chess board, a giant checkers set, a rock wall, and an inflatable dinosaur for our after-prom suggestions so far."

2. Be sure that everyone in attendance understands the suggestions.

   "Remember, the inflatable dinosaur would be ridden — sort of like a mechanical bull.

3. If duplicate ideas are offered, write them down and sort them out later.

   "A giant chess board is pretty similar to a giant checkers set, so let's combine the two ideas."

4. Encourage people to give any and all suggestions that come to mind.

   "I think the inflatable dinosaur would be cool, but I think we should make sure that we use a dinosaur that stays close to the ground and doesn't eat meat."

5. If you feel that you have all the ideas, let it rest, and ask for more suggestions a little later. If the participants are still coming up with

a lot of ideas, keep going. You can sort through and eliminate useless ideas later.

"Thanks for the suggestions everybody! I don't think we'll be cloning dinosaurs to ride them like horses anytime soon, but I think this meeting has been really productive. It's time for a donut break!"

3

Different Kinds of Communication

The meetings we discussed in the last chapter are usually conducted with people seated face-to-face in a room. However, if you need to meet with people and don't have time to hold a proper meeting, you can use other methods of communication.

Email

As you might imagine, email is a great way to send announcements, distribute information, or request that people send their thoughts about particular questions or concerns. You can also conduct a meeting through email. Meeting participants can share information, thoughts, opinions, and suggestions. It's a great way to circulate your questions and give people a chance to think about the answers before responding.

Fast Fact ═══════════════════════════

Over one billion emails are sent per day (**www.radicati.com**).

Email is free and so easy to use that people use it too frequently. Back in the olden days, if someone received a letter, they might respond once. Now, you can send trivial emails back and forth for hours. It's way more practical to send an email only when you have something useful to say. Think before sending, because if you keep forgetting everything you wanted to say in one email, other members of the chain might get annoyed with you.

Email etiquette

Just like saying "please" and "thank you" at the dinner table, using email has its own set of manners. Because you can't hear the tone of voice through text, be sure to write exactly what you mean before you send an email.

Here are some other email etiquette tips:

- Avoid "flaming," a personal attack through words whether spoken, written, or typed.

- Delete unimportant information. Though you might think it's important to talk about Kanye's new album, other members of your group might not be as big of fans of "Yeezus."

- When you respond to an email, include only the relevant parts of the message, and use a descriptive subject. When you respond to an email, the subject line should be preceded by "RE:" and should remain the same. However, when the subject of any email changes, it's a good idea to change the subject line. This is really useful when you are reviewing saved emails to find something specific.

- Be clear and careful. Be sure you understand the message before you respond.

- DO NOT USE ALL CAPS. It is perceived as yelling, and is considered rude. And try not to use sarcasm; it's hard to understand through text, and others may get confused by what you really mean.

Common email mistakes to avoid

1. Typing the message in the subject line instead of in the body.

   "I thought 'Hey Y'all What's Up' was a weird title for an email!"

2. Using imprecise language that can be misinterpreted.

   "So you know about the 'thing' we talked about yesterday? I think that 'thing' was a stupid idea. Let's forget the 'thing.'"

3. Not signing off before leaving the computer, allowing others to use your email address.

"Hey, who sent an email to the principal and told her I lost all use of my fingers and needed to resign from prom committee? Not cool!"

4. Not checking email thoroughly and missing something important.

"Oh, I thought the meeting next week was in the gym, not the library! No wonder the basketball team thought it was weird I was watching them play!"

5. Forgetting your password.

"Is it IloveDoNuts123 or IloveDonuts321?"

6. Sending messages to the wrong email address.

"Sorry, Mom. I know you're not interested in the prom..."

The good thing about email meetings is that they allow each participant to have a written copy of all suggestions, questions, and ideas. Here are some things to remember with your email meeting contributions:

- Keep your posts short. Short sentences and paragraphs can be read quickly.

- Focus on only one subject per message, and use an appropriate subject line.

- Write your name at the beginning of each post so there isn't any confusion about who submitted the idea.

- Your comments should be at the top of the page, not worked into the existing text.

Another nice thing about email meetings is that almost everyone is familiar with how they work. Remember that some people check their email infrequently, and you might need to be patient with them. If you would like a simple way to notify people that they have an email, you can download **www.eprompter.com**, a program that checks all your email accounts every 15 minutes and notifies you when there are messages.

If some participants are hesitant to join in the discussion, the leader should send them a reminder to nudge them to get involved. Other participants may respond to every message sent, but don't let these eager beavers and their excessive activity mask the fact that others may not be participating. When some of your group members are concerned about getting their point across in writing, encourage them simply to state what is on their mind. They don't need to get fancy with their wording. The encouraging thing is that their comfort level will rise with practice.

Online Message Groups

If email is too old school for you or you need quick responses, there are other good technological options for you. These instant messenger apps allow you to hold text meetings with as many people as you like and are useful if you need to get in touch with members of your group quickly. However, both require that you have an account, and if members of your group don't have one, they will be left out of the message.

Facebook™ Messenger

Facebook Messenger is an instant messaging service from the social media website Facebook™. You can send messages to others, as well as pictures and voice communication. Messenger is available on mobile phones and on Facebook's main website.

Fast Fact

Facebook has 1.65 billion monthly active users around the world as of March 31, 2016 (**www.cnn.com**).

Google Chat™

Similar to Facebook Messenger, Google Chat is an instant messaging service through text and voice communication. It is also known as "gtalk" or "gmessage."

Virtual Meeting Options

If you want to talk to members of your group face-to-face but can't meet in person, a good webcam and the right tools can go a long way. Isn't the 21st century great?

Skype™

One great option for a virtual meeting is Skype. Skype is an app that lets its users chat with others through a webcam and microphone. Skype users can exchange images, text, video, and can also do video conference calls. It is available for Microsoft and Apple products, as well as Android, Blackberry, and Linux products. Skype-to-Skype calls are free of charge, which makes it an ideal app for a group meeting. You can download Skype via the iTunes store.

Google Hangouts™

Another useful way of connecting with others is Google Hangouts. Google Hangouts, created by Google, allows up to 10 users to meet virtually via text, voice, or video chats. Hangouts are built into the Google+™ social network and Gmail™, and mobile apps are also available for iOS™ and Android™ devices on the iTunes° store.

Fast Fact

There are more than 2 million Google searches per second (**www. businessinsider.com**).

Other Helpful Apps

Applications, or "apps," are available to anyone with a smart phone or a computer. There's an app for anything you can think of, including games, cooking, sports — and yes, meetings.

Minute

Minute specializes in paperless meetings and to-do lists, and is ideal for busy members of your group or organization. This free app allows you to turn agenda appointments into meetings, invite attendees, and import and share important documents. All agenda items are in a single place, so members of your organization can view documents easily. You can also directly delegate tasks as well as read and revise notes and create the next meeting with a single press of a button. This app is available from the iTunes store.

Anywhere Pad

Anywhere Pad—also known as Azeus Convene—is a board meeting app for both face-to-face and digital meetings. Downloading Anywhere Pad allows members access to an online portal where meetings can be organized, documents can be prepared, and members can brainstorm and discuss ideas on whiteboards. Anywhere Pad is available for Android mobile devices.

MeetingBurner

Do you and your group need to meet face-to-face but can't seem to find time? Meeting Burner is a free app that lets you host online meetings and webinars. Participants can join meetings with their iOS device, and it gives them access to meeting information, screen sharing, chat, participant lists, streaming audio, and more. You can find this app on the iTunes store.

4

The Details of Your Meetings

You know the type of meeting you want to hold. Now, it's time to figure out the finer details. We'll discuss these details by calling them the "what," "who," and "when" of your meeting.

What Will Happen?

What information will need to be discussed, or which problems need to be solved? Making a list or an outline helps participants be prepared to stay on the subject and avoid rambling discussions.

Do you need regularly scheduled meetings? Some groups have meetings automatically scheduled for a specific day and time, but be sure to only do this if you know your group will always need to meet. There is nothing worse than attending a meeting that isn't really necessary. You can ask yourself these questions to find whether the meeting is necessary.

Is the meeting necessary? The official checklist

1. Is anything gained by holding the meeting?

   Yes   **No**

2. Is anything lost by not holding the meeting?

   Yes   **No**

3. Would an email accomplish the same thing?

   Yes   **No**

4. Could you schedule fewer meetings and accomplish just as much?

   Yes   **No**

5. Do participants have enough time to prepare?

   Yes   **No**

6. Do you really want input on the situation or problem?

   Yes   **No**

7. How will the meeting purpose affect the participants?

   Yes   **No**

8. Are you positive someone will bring donuts to this meeting?4

   Yes   **No**

---

4. Again, not a *totally* necessary requirement for a meeting . . . but it can't hurt!

Once you have established that you *do* need to meet, you'll want to form a specific purpose or goal that you want to accomplish when you meet. Here are some common purposes for meetings. Do any of them fit your plans?

- To give announcements and status reports

  "The Donut Enthusiast club has about half of its budget left for the entire year!"

- To share results (committee reports)

  "We've polled the school, and the results are in — more people love chocolate donuts than vanilla donuts."

- To offer presentations on subjects that will interest participants

  "Hannah will now speak on the importance of donuts in any business meeting."

- To coordinate projects, schedules, and group or individual assignments

  "When can we get together to make donuts?"

- To offer training or the chance to learn new skills and procedures

  "There will be a donut-making class next week in the art room!"

- To set goals and objectives and to develop strategies to accomplish them

  "We want to give out donuts to the entire school next month — we're calling it Operation Donut."

- To solve problems, analyze issues and ideas, and discuss possible solutions

  "Should we surprise the entire school or tell everyone in advance?"

- To make decisions, to evaluate situations and options, and to gain a consensus

  "I think Operation Donut should be a surprise—what do you think?"

- To socialize and take time to get to know each other

  "On the count of three, everyone yell out his or her favorite kind of donut!"

- To build a team that will motivate and inspire members

  "Donut party at my house next week!"

Most meetings involve problem solving and bringing staff members together to generate ideas and to find creative solutions, but your meeting can have more than one purpose. You can also incorporate ongoing purposes in your meeting. Some ongoing purposes include:

- Building a team

  "As President of the Donut Enthusiast Club, I want members to feel included and happy (and full of donuts) throughout the semester."

- Improving safety practices

  "By the end of the year, I want members to know how to create donuts safely in their own homes."

- Increasing productivity

  "In general, I want members to be enthusiastic and willing to work in the Donut Enthusiast Club."

- Increasing employee knowledge

  "I want members to know everything there is to know about donuts."

- Building leadership skills

"Younger members should be able to speak up, feel included, and be able to bake their own donuts by the end of the semester."

These are only a few of the possible purposes that you can incorporate into your meetings.

A clear purpose is the first step for an effective and successful meeting!

Know Your Purpose

"Why are we here?" is probably the most common question asked during a meeting, followed shortly by "When can we leave?" People want to know why they are in a situation—and that includes meetings. Your peers might not ask you directly, but they are probably asking themselves or other people why they are at the meeting. It is critical that you have an answer to that question. These are some examples of things you should and should *not* say to meeting attendees.

Bad things to say at your meeting

- "We are here today since we haven't had a meeting in over seven months."

- "I forgot to tell you that we have an event tomorrow."

- "I have over 30 new ideas on ways to restructure the Donut Enthusiast club, and I'm going to tell you all of them right now."

Yikes, right? Let's reword these thoughts.

Good things to say at your meeting

- "We are meeting because I need the details on the progress of 'Operation Donut.'"

- "We need to discuss a new Donut Enthusiast Club event that will happen next month."

- "We are here to discuss some ideas to restructure the Donut Enthusiast Club, and I need your thoughts and suggestions."

Next, consider whether this meeting is to get or to give information. Remember to list the information you will share, and as you create the list, be realistic.

- Is the purpose something that you can accomplish?

- Do you have the information handy that the attendees of the meeting need?

- Do you personally understand this information?

- Do attendees already have the information they need?

- Is there enough time to discuss and handle the subject?

- Did you invite the right people to the meeting to accomplish the purpose?

- Do you have the authority to see the purpose through to a conclusion?

- Did you invite the person who does have the authority if you don't?

- Have you thoroughly prepared for the meeting?

If the answers to all of these questions is a confident "Yes!" then you are ready to make your purpose known!

Make the purpose known

It is normal for our minds to imagine terrible possibilities if we don't know what is happening. For example, if you set up a meeting for the Donut Enthusiast Club but don't tell them why you are meeting, they may think it is because you are disbanding the club, and they may begin to panic.

Attendees need to understand the purpose for the meeting. This lets them prepare and participate more fully. Even when the purpose is confidential, your peers should be told *something*. Otherwise, you may lose control of the meeting in their rush to ask questions.

Tell others about the purpose

No matter how well you prepare, you cannot bring a random subject to the table and expect attendees to understand it right off the bat. How can they prepare any information or prepare mentally if they don't even know what the meeting will be about? They need enough time to do any research or preparation before the meeting.

To prepare, attendees need specific information such as:

- **Subject and Purpose**: You do not need to outline every single detail, but the few minutes you take to explain will save everyone time at the meeting. For example, let members of the Donut Enthusiast Club know that you are meeting to plan next year's budget.

- **An Agenda**: Include the specific information you plan to cover on your agenda. If part of the meeting includes eating donuts, remember to document it on your agenda so members of the Donut Enthusiast Club come ready to eat delicious pastries!

Even if you're planning a meeting for your theatre club, remember to forgo the drama: Do not leave things off to get a reaction. Tell attendees exactly what will be covered. When you spring unexpected topics on the participants, they will not respond positively.

A few words about agendas

An agenda is like a roadmap to get your meeting from point A to point B based on where you want to start the meeting and where you will lead the attendees. Your agenda needs to be clear, specific, and brief.

Fast Fact

Meeting participants consider 34 percent of a meeting to be useless (**http://attentiv.com**).

Let's say the Donut Enthusiast Club wants to offer a scholarship. The agenda can say that the members of the club will consider a scholarship, or it can say that members of the club will discuss how to choose applicants to receive a scholarship from the Donut Enthusiast Club. Do you see the difference in these two approaches?

Agenda Guidelines

- **Reveal Your Expectations**—You need to tell meeting attendees what you expect from them ahead of time. If you want comments about specific agenda items, tell them. When you need someone to contribute to a specific topic, make this known when you invite them or when you send them a copy of the agenda. If their contribution regards research or compilation of information, they'll need enough time to assemble the details you need.

- **Meeting Details: When and Where** — Meeting attendees need to know when the meeting will be, where it will be, and how long it will last. This information requires advance planning to secure a site or meeting room, to make sure attendees are available, and to provide enough time to cover the agenda.

You also want to avoid sending someone the agenda ten minutes before the meeting start time. They won't have time to look over it and will not be able to contribute fully!

Think your agenda is ready to go? When you notify attendees about the meeting, keep the following list in mind:

1. **Write It Down**: Say it with me: "Compose and communicate." Do not expect people to remember the details. It is much more effective to send a quick email or text with the information.

2. **Preparation Time**: Keep in mind that students are always busy with homework and other after-school activities. Do not put rush attendees to prepare their contributions by telling them about the agenda minutes before the meeting!

3. **Confirmation**: You, or someone helping you, should make sure that all invited attendees received their notification and information about the meeting. This should take only a moment or two to confirm they received the information and read it.

Remember, it will help your organization to make sure all potential attendees are notified and can be prepared for your meetings.

Avoid ulterior motives

Take a close look at your plans and purpose to confirm that the agenda has no fuzzy language. Have you listed Operation Donut on your agenda, but you plan to discuss Donut Making 101 for the majority of the meeting?

Fast Fact

Call a point of order when someone is disobeying the rules of the meeting (**www.robertsrules.org**).

ROBERT'S RULES QUICK REFERENCE:
How to Rise to a Point of Order

Why would I want to do this?

You would choose to raise a point of order if the rules are not being followed.

- Without being called on, you say, **"I rise to a point of order,"** or **"Point of order."**

Quick notes:

Can I interrupt the speaker? **Yes.** Second needed? **No.** Debatable? **No.** Amendable? **No.**

Vote needed? **Chair decides.**

If you're new at leading meetings, you may be able to get away with this—once. If you don't follow the agenda, it will make your attendees feel that you are unprepared or incompetent. Your more experienced members will spot the problem, and it will mess up the flow of the meeting and the effectiveness of your leadership. When a leader is honest and direct, others are encouraged to give honest feedback and suggestions and to ask good questions. You will have created an atmosphere more conducive to learning and accomplishing your tasks.

Who Will You Invite?

It's important to know who you want at your meeting. For example, if you want to hold a meeting for members of the Donut Enthusiast Club who have volunteered to bake donuts for the entire school, you'll want to make sure that you invite all people who you think would be beneficial to the meeting.

When you're considering who to invite to your meeting, there are three categories to think about:

- People who should attend

- People who shouldn't attend

- Those whose absence would cause you to consider rescheduling

---

ROBERT'S RULES QUICK REFERENCE:
Things to Keep in Mind When Debating

- No matter how right you think you are, listen to the opposing argument.

- Keep the issue at the forefront.

- Prepare for counterargument.

- Be considerate!

Still confused? Say you're trying to decide if you should invite Jerry to a Donut Enthusiast meeting where you'll be discussing the Annual Donut Bake Sale. Here's a handy checklist to see if Jerry should attend the meeting.

Should I invite Jerry to the donut bake sale meeting?

1. Will Jerry help you accomplish your goal of baking donuts for the entire school?

    Yes   **No**

2. Does Jerry have a special interest in baking donuts?

    Yes   **No**

3. Does Jerry have the power to approve and implement changes?

    Yes   **No**

4. Does Jerry have particular information on baking donuts?

    Yes   **No**

5. Will Jerry give a presentation that will be helpful?

Yes   **No**

6. Is Jerry a creative problem solver?

Yes   **No**

7. Does Jerry need additional training for baking donuts?

Yes   **No**

If you answered "Yes" to one or more of these questions, you definitely should invite Jerry to your meeting. But what if Jerry is kind of a jerk, and you aren't sure if he should attend the meeting? Stop right there—if Jerry is a member of your group or organization, according to Robert's Rules, he has the same right as anyone else to attend. You can step away from Robert's Rules and deny Jerry the right to attend, but that means you are no longer holding a meeting that reflects the age-old traditions. (It's also not fair.)

Fast Fact

When someone is speaking very quietly during a meeting, call a point of personal privilege—it asks that member to speak up! (**www.robertsrules.org**).

ROBERT'S RULES QUICK REFERENCE:
How to Raise a Point of Personal Privilege

Why would I want to do this?

You would choose to do so if it is too noisy outside the meeting, the room temperature is not comfortable, etc.

- Without recognition, you say, **"Point of personal privilege."**

- The chairperson would say, **"State your point."**

- You would follow with, **"There is too much noise,"** or **"It's too hot in here,"** etc.

Quick notes:

Can I interrupt the speaker? **Yes.** Second needed? **No.** Debatable? **No.** Amendable? **No.**

Vote needed? **Chair decides.**

What if Jerry is supposed to go to the meeting, and he can't make it? Maybe you should consider rescheduling. Consider these four points before you decide to change the time, date, and place of your meeting.

1. Does Jerry want to hear the donut discussion?

Yes   No

2. Could Jerry influence the outcome of the meeting?

Yes   No

3. Can you connect with Jerry through a phone or video conference?

Yes   No

4. Will Jerry have enough time to prepare for the meeting?

Yes   **No**

If the answer is "Yes" to one of those questions, do your best to work around Jerry's scheduling issue. If his voice in your organization is integral to your progress, other members will thank you and will gladly reschedule.

Part-time attendees

Are there members of your organization who don't need to be involved in the entire meeting? For example, if you're training new members on proper procedure of Donut Making 101, you might not need the guest donut baker to attend the entire meeting. During networking meetings in the business world, the schedule can work like this:

- President – Attends entire meeting

- Vice President – Attends entire meeting

- Secretary/Treasurer – Attends entire meeting

- Training Supervisor – Attends the portion of the meeting that involves his or her duties

- Guest Hosts – Attends the portion of the meeting that involves their duties

The president, vice president, and secretary/treasurer need to attend all sessions, because any of them could be requested to conduct a meeting. The other positions only require specialized training for their particular area, and the only sessions that they have to attend are the ones focusing on their expertise.

Fast Fact ────────────────────────────────

When you want to ask the speaker a question, it is generally best to call a point of information (**www.robertsrules.org**).

ROBERT'S RULES QUICK REFERENCE:
How to Get More Information

Really, why would I want to do this?

You would do so if you want more facts or information dealing with a discussion.

- Without recognition, you say, **"Point of information."**

Quick notes:

Can I interrupt the speaker? **Yes.** Second needed? **No.** Debatable? **No.** Amendable? **No.**

Vote needed? **None.**

How many people should attend my meeting?

There isn't a magic number that determines how many people should attend a meeting; that totally depends on the type of meeting being held. I provided some guidelines in Chapter 2 about the size of the meeting based on the type, but in general, you need enough people to accomplish your goals without having additional people just sitting around.

Pretty vague, right?

You can use smaller groups for idea and feedback discussions. If you start out with a larger group, those people can be broken into smaller groups. The smaller groups can discuss ideas and suggestions and report to the larger group. This is a great way to use a large number of people for generating ideas and solving problems.

Another option is to have a smaller meeting before the main meeting. This would include group members who represent the larger group. The smaller group can discuss particular details that do not need to be discussed with the entire group. It is easier to interact with the smaller group, and you will not have to tie up the large group on unnecessary details. This is a great idea for an officer board or the executive members of your organization.

But how do you decide how big your group should be?

First, you need to ask yourself how many people are really needed to accomplish the goals for your meeting. This is one of the reasons we discussed figuring out the purpose of your meeting first. Decide what you need to accomplish, and then you can decide who to involve and how many people to include from there.

Here are some general guidelines on how many people should be attending your meetings.

Two to Eight Attendees

This number is good for a small group with the president leading the meeting, like an officer board. Do all people in the club or organization need to attend all of the meetings? If not, two to eight attendees might be a good idea.

A small meeting should be prepared just like a normal meeting. You probably won't need someone to lead the group, but you'll want to have a plan for what needs to be accomplished. An agenda will still be needed for each attendee so members can prepare and participate.

When the group is only a few people, an argument can start between two or more meeting attendees. If this happens, one of the other members needs to step in to avoid losing control of the meeting. It is also easier to go off track: If Jerry drifts off subject during his explanation of Donut Enthusiast Club funds, someone needs to speak up to get the meeting back on track. There may also be times when the meeting becomes emotionally charged, or everyone is intimately involved. It is best to end the meeting and give the attendees a chance to calm down before discussing the topics further.

Eight to 15 Attendees

This is a great size for problem-solving meetings. This number of people allows each person to participate and gives everyone a chance to hear what others think. The smaller size gives you to option to keep the meeting informal. It's fine to be informal, but you still need a clear purpose and structure for the most effective meeting.

15-30 Attendees

You do *not* need this many people for most meetings. When you have this many people, you cannot problem solve as well, and participation has to be limited. However, if you want to share information, this many attendees might be best.

More than 30 Attendees

Large groups are best for lectures, panel discussions, formal debates, and conducting a vote. If people are going to participate, there must be rules, and they must be enforced. Parliamentary procedure and Robert's Rules are usually best suited for larger groups. Earlier, we discussed the possibility of breaking large meetings into smaller groups to gather problem-solving feedback. When you decide to do this, have definite suggestions about how the small groups will operate and what they need to accomplish. An experienced leader should also roam among the participants to ensure they accomplish things and to answer questions that might arise.[5]

Group attitudes and behaviors to avoid

Have you ever been at a meeting where everyone agrees and nobody has a dissenting opinion? While it may move the meeting along, it can actually

---

5. You'll also have to bring a lot of donuts.

be harmful. Psychologist Irving L. Janis calls this tendency of a group to think alike "groupthink."

Fast Fact

Events in history such as the 2008 financial crisis and the disastrous 1961 Bay of Pigs invasion are attributed to groupthink and the inability to foresee problems (**www. communicationstudies.com**).

Groupthink occurs when your organization needs to make a decision. Sometimes, others will ignore people who disagree with them, and in these cases, the majority opinion can steamroll over the minority. Some meetings are often conducted using different rules when there is unusual pressure to make a decision. The decisions reached in these situations may not reflect the honest feelings and beliefs of the participants. After one decision is made in a group with this kind of mentality, they find it even easier to make other bad decisions in the same way.

Fast Fact

Groupthink is seen everywhere, but it is especially noted in politics, sports, the corporate world, and religious cults (**www. icsahome.com**).

If you're not sure if your group suffers from groupthink, here is a guide to spotting the beginning signs at your meeting.

The official groupthink guide

1. **Warning Sign:** Do you see some members of the meeting agreeing with other people even if that doesn't reflect their thoughts, beliefs, and experiences?

   The Cure: Make it clear that you welcome *all* viewpoints and suggestions.

2. **Warning Sign:** Does someone in authority believe he or she is always right?

   The Cure: Remind members of your group that just because someone is in charge does not mean he or she has the right opinion.

3. **Warning Sign:** Do older members of your group ignore younger members' ideas?

   The Cure: Make it clear that clinging to certain thoughts, beliefs, and ideas is not a productive way to work and will limit the effectiveness of the group.

4. **Warning Sign:** Do group members in positions of power ignore more general members of your organization?

   The Cure: Remind older members what it was like to be in the organization before they received leadership positions.

5. **Warning Sign:** Do younger members of your organization feel pressured to go along with older members and leaders?

   The Cure: Make it clear that leaders should definitely participate in your meetings, but their ideas should not squelch other opinions.

All groups need to try and avoid these problems. It is a mentality that can make your meetings ineffective no matter how much planning you do. Keep communication open with all participants, and invite people who can represent each side of an issue.

Fast Fact

One recommended way of curing groupthink is to play "devil's advocate" and look at the problem from a different point of view (**http://oregonstate.edu**).

When Will Your Meeting Happen?

The right meeting time can make a big difference in the attendance, the participation, and the productivity of your meeting. Some days of the week are also better for meetings. Fridays might be a bad time for people who like to enjoy every minute of their weekend, and Mondays could mean less enthusiasm and participation. The worst times to conduct meetings include late afternoons before holidays or weekends and early mornings after holidays or weekends.

Fast Fact

On an average day, there are 25 million meetings in America (**www.themuse.com**).

Here are some things you need to consider:

- When are you available?

- When will you be prepared?

- When are members of your group available?

- When is the meeting place available?

- How long will it take to prepare the meeting place?

A meeting during lunch in a quiet room might be a good idea if there isn't a time before or after school, but most groups and organizations meet before or after school hours. Weekday evenings and afternoons are some of the only possibilities. Some groups may even need to meet on Saturday morning or Sunday afternoon. However, there isn't an unacceptable time if the building is available and the attendees are in agreement. You can use a day planner to figure which days or time would be better for your meeting.

5

Planning 101

You know the kind of meeting you want to hold. You know the purpose and goals of your meeting. You even know the "who," "what," and "when" of your meeting. You're well on your way to becoming a meeting planner superhero, but now it's time to dig deeper and talk about something different: the plan of action.

Planning meetings ahead of time are helpful, but where do you even start?

Begin to Plan

Say you're the president of the student council, and you and your group have decided that the big event of the year will be a donut-themed scavenger hunt . . . but that's all you've accomplished. As the president, you're feeling a little stressed—the next meeting is on Friday, and how do you even begin to plan it?

Here's a 15-step list to help you plan your meeting to make sure everything is on track.

Fifteen steps to plan a meeting

1. **Determine the purpose and desired outcome**

   You'll want to determine the points you want to talk about and the actions you want to take at your meeting. If the next step on the Donut Scavenger Hunt planning list is to determine the budget, write down all that you want to discuss and the results you should have when you've ended the meeting.

2. **Establish boundaries for the meeting**

   After you've established the purpose and outcome, decide how the meeting will begin and end. Do you want to let other members know that the goal of your meeting has been met? Do you want to start planning another meeting with your group? Do you want to begin or end the meeting with donuts? These kinds of questions allow you to structure the meeting in a way that is more useful.

3. **Determine the meeting objectives**

    Pick three to six goals based on the meeting purpose. What actions need to be taken to accomplish these goals? If you're planning the budget of a delicious scavenger hunt during the meeting, maybe you'll want to decide the kinds of clues, prizes, and other money you'll need for the planning of the event.

4. **Figure out who is in charge and will make sure the goals are met**

    Think about the people in Student Council with you and the roles they fulfill in the meeting planning process. Who will be responsible to see that the goals are met by the end of the meeting? Who will oversee the meeting and make sure everyone is on track? What happens if the goals during this meeting are not met?

5. **Choose effective agenda points**

    Choose the main things that must be done to accomplish these goals. If you're figuring out the budget for the scavenger hunt, maybe you'd want to start off the meeting talking about how much money the group can spend on the event.

6. **Process the necessary information**

    Do you have access to the information that you need? Does it need to be organized? Do you need help organizing the materials? Thinking about the necessary information will save a lot of hassle during the meeting.

7. **Use effective tools**

    What tools will be used to assemble the information? Think about the kinds of equipment you'll need — for example, if you want to use a visual chart to talk about the budget, you'll have to set up the computer program beforehand.

8. Take responsibility

Someone needs to be responsible for each item in the meeting. Sometimes, you only need one or two people, but at other times, you'll need to assign a task to the group. Think about how many people are needed and find the right people or person to handle each item.

9. Timeframe for the meeting

Decide how long you want to talk about each item on your agenda. This will allow your meeting to run smoothly and make sure you and your group don't talk about one subject for too long.

10. Decide what roles are needed and who will fill them

Who will be at the meeting? Will you need a secretary? Presenters? Your own personal chef? In a smaller meeting, you don't need to assign each of these roles, but it is best to assign roles when you have more members attending your meeting.

11. Establish the logistical needs for your meeting

Although it may seem obvious, you'll have to decide on the location, time, and day for the meeting. This should also include information about how long the meeting will last so members of your organization can plan accordingly.

12. Assemble the needed materials

What materials are needed? These materials could include handouts, charts, graphs, chalkboards, white boards, projectors . . . the choice is yours. How should the materials be presented to maximize their effectiveness for the attendees?

13. **Establish appropriate ground rules**

    Imagine how annoying it would be if Jerry the Jerk keeps yelling out suggestions without raising his hand or playing solitaire on his phone instead of paying attention? Although this may already be in your organization's constitution, you need to make sure everyone will follow the ground rules. This will allow your meeting to run smoothly — and save you from yelling yourself hoarse at Jerry.

14. **Acceptable actions**

    You and members of your group must agree on the steps to be taken when planning your events, developing a plan of action, planning any additional meetings, and any other necessary changes in the way business is done in your meetings.

15. **Receiving feedback**

    If this is your first time running a meeting, it's a good idea to have other members of your organization evaluate your role as a leader. Asking them to fill out a survey to evaluate the meeting, the flow of information, the various roles and how they were handled, and the outcome of the meeting can help you improve your leadership skills. Make sure to emphasize in your survey that an evaluation should not just indicate there are problems — you will also want suggestions on how to improve future meetings.

Agendas

You've got a million problems to solve when you're planning the Annual Donut Scavenger Hunt, but don't try to tackle them all at one meeting. Your agenda will work better if you only bring up a small number of problems. If you try to focus on too many things, you will not accomplish much, and attendees will be distracted by too many topics.

Pre-meeting

1. **State your purpose, goals, and the agenda**

   Try this at the beginning of the meeting. This is the perfect time to be sure that the participants and attendees understand why you're having the meeting and why they were invited.

2. **Determine the roles for participants and explain their responsibilities**

   Understand individual roles and how certain duties work into the agenda. Who takes notes? Who is in charge of the budget? Who brings the snacks? Have you explained the responsibilities to each person?

3. **Choose the method for making decisions**

   Say you're trying to make a decision about the kinds of donuts you'll serve for refreshments at the scavenger hunt. Did you know there's a whole slew of different procedures to reach a verdict? Some of these include:

   • Voting to find a majority

   • Voting that needs a two-thirds, three-fourths, or higher number to reach a decision

   • Referring information and decision to a portion of the group

   • Reaching a consensus with additional considerations

   • Reaching a consensus without additional considerations

4. **Additional ideas**

   Any group of people is probably going to come up with ideas that are good, but not for the current project. When this happens, have a procedure to write them down and to review them later, helping you to save the idea while still working to keep the meeting on track. You can schedule a time near the end of the meeting to discuss these items and possibly decide which things to add to future agendas. If it's something simple and you have time, you can address the idea.

During the meeting

1. Set the tone

The leader of the meeting needs to set the correct tone from the beginning. Being friendly and cheerful can be a great start. Acknowledge people when they enter, and be helpful. And if you can, tell a joke! (Example: "I used to be on a diet, but I donut care anymore!"[6]) You don't have to be a stand-up comedian, but a sense of humor leads to a group that is more relaxed and willing to take on projects.

2. Introduction

It might be good to offer a brief overview of the group and the reason it was formed along with some of its accomplishments. This is especially helpful when you have visitors.

3. Build your team

Some groups need to work on becoming a team. If your group is not cohesive, you can plan some team-building exercises so members are more comfortable with each other.

4. Tasks or projects

The main reason for having a meeting is to make a decision, find a solution, or to accomplish some other task. This objective needs to be addressed clearly.

5. The next step

Have a list or chart that shows what should be done next and who will take this action.

6. Closing

Like a book, movie, or TV show, a bad ending can ruin a good story. A meeting is no exception — it needs a clear signal that it's over. There are several ways to conclude a meeting. Which of these ideas are right for your group?

---

6. Look, I never said it had to be a *good* joke!

- Review any decisions.

  "We've decided to spend $400 of our annual budget on the Donut Scavenger Hunt."

- Clearly state the next steps to be taken.

  "At the next meeting, we'll discuss the prizes for the Donut Scavenger Hunt."

- Review additional ideas that were mentioned.

  "We really liked Jerry's idea about a giant pool filled with jelly donuts on the football field."

- Evaluate the meeting along with suggested ways to improve.

  "Let's try to keep the discussion on chocolate vs. vanilla donuts to a minimum, shall we?"

- Find a personal way to close the meeting.

  "Have a good night, everybody! As my grandmother once said, ''Donut' worry about what others think of you!'"

---

7. Okay, I'll admit it — my grandmother never said this.

CASE STUDY: JANET M. NAST

Author, IT Trainer, and Tech Writer
www.janetmnast.com

Over my 40-year career, I've attended and facilitated many meetings, and none went more smoothly than the ones that were organized with an agenda and three key roles that I learned from my last employer. Here are some tips to make sure your meetings are as productive as possible:

Create an agenda

An effective agenda should include the following information:

- A list of topics (agenda items)

- The name of the person to lead the discussion for each topic

- Any materials or information that each person is expected to prepare and present

- The amount of time allowed for each topic—this prevents a meeting from running late, and it allows an appropriate amount of time for each topic to be discussed

- The expected outcome of each discussion—stating an expected outcome of any discussion helps people to stay focused on a common goal and to not get side tracked or talk for the sake of talking

Here are a couple of agenda item examples:

1. Create the initial task assignment list

2. Hammer out the timeline for each task

The meeting facilitator or the person requesting the meeting should create the agenda. Ideally, both people would create it so that the topics can be prioritized by at least two of the meeting's leaders.

Who creates the agenda is not critical so long as there is one and it is sent to all participants a few days before the meeting. This way, all participants have some time to prepare information that might be required of them for the meeting. At the very least, it will give everyone time to think of information they might be able to contribute to the discussion. Nothing wastes more time than someone showing up unprepared and then everyone having to sit around waiting for him or her to get his or her act together.

Specify these three roles for every meeting:

1. The facilitator: This is the person who begins each meeting by reviewing the agenda and asking if there are any other topics that need to be discussed (if time permits).

He or she will then introduce each topic, the time allowed for each topic, the expected outcome, and then share any pertinent information that will get the discussion moving.

This is also the same person who keeps the discussion on topic. We've all been in meetings where someone makes a comment about a subject and it triggers a whole other side discussion between one or two people. This can very disruptive, and it's a waste of everyone else's time. The facilitator will be the one to stop the meeting and ask if this is another topic that needs to be added to the next meeting's agenda, or possibly critical enough to be discussed here and now. In that case, he will decide if there is time to do so by rescheduling one of the other agenda items into the next meeting.

2. Time keeper: This person keeps things moving. He or she refers to a printed out copy of the agenda to watch the clock and then lets everyone know when the group is running out of time for said topic. The time keeper will work very closely with the facilitator in this role. He or she might need to say, "We have one minute left for this topic. Would you like to continue this discussion, which might not leave us room for the last item on the agenda, or table it for the next meeting?" (I've seen some time keepers set alarms on their smart phones.)

3. Note taker: This person not only takes general notes on each topic discussion, but he or she keeps track of action items that come up, whom they are assigned to, and the expected completion dates. At the end of the meeting, these notes should be typed up and emailed to each meeting participant. That way, everyone knows what is expected of him or her as a result of the meeting.

For those who were invited but couldn't attend the meeting for whatever reason, the notes need to be emailed to them. That way, all of the people involved are aware of what happened while they were gone, and if tasks were assigned to any of them, those people have time to get it done. If the absent person expects to be out of commission for longer than anticipated by the team, he or she will also have the opportunity to let the meeting facilitator know, and then the task can be reassigned.

Sometimes, a meeting might not have enough attendees for each role to be assigned to a different person. In that case, there should still always be a facilitator; and I've seen many facilitators perform all three roles.

In my experience, when these roles were in place, every single meeting ran efficiently, decisions were made, tasks were assigned, and things got done—every single time. There was no wasting time on side subjects because the facilitators and timekeepers didn't allow it. The people attending the meetings appreciated this structure, because they all knew it would not be another typical meeting where one person dominated the whole thing and everyone else lost interest.

Janet M. Nast is the author of "Shifting to the Business of Life," and is an IT trainer and tech writer. You can follow her on Twitter (@janetmnast) or visit her website at www.janetmnast.com.

Fast Fact

Sorry, boys. A recent study by the Harvard Business Review found that women had the higher group intelligence (**www.businessinsider.com**).

Prepping ideas

Have you been to meetings where leaders are nervous and stumble over their words? What about when participants who aren't sure what the meeting is about and never speak up? Planning is essential for a successful meeting, but there are many different ways to prepare. Which one works best for you?

Team or solo preparation

Sometimes, it can be easier to prepare the meeting alone, because you don't need to work with other people and can plan the meeting quickly. However, if it's a large or complex meeting, it might be a good idea to consult with others for help in organizing all the elements of the meeting.

These are some of the reasons you would want to include others in your preparation:

- Use their creativity and get their input on the plans and agenda

- Portions of the preparation can be delegated to qualified people[8]

- Attendees will feel more involved in the process and will do more to make the meeting effective

---

8. It is a really bad idea to delegate tasks to unqualified or unmotivated people.

- This can train members of your organization and increase their leadership skills

Ground rules

Ground rules need to be established before the meeting, and all members need to understand the rules. If not, the meeting can easily fall apart. For example, one simple rule is that only one person should speak at a time and that people must raise their hands to speak. The meeting leader will then call on people to speak.

These ground rules can also include such things as:

- Explain how the meeting leader will behave

- Outline any specific information about behavior of meeting attendees

- Determine the procedure to present agenda items

- Decide how subjects will be introduced and discussed

- Create a way to collect and evaluate information

- Decide how disruptions and problems in the meeting will be handled

- Decide that meetings will begin and end on time

Many people refer to Robert's Rules of Order, but they may not really understand the rules or they may just think they have to refer to it. Any rules that you plan to use need to be reviewed to be sure that they are effective. When you consider making changes, try new rules with the group and then adopt them once you know they work.

Remember not to implement too many rules at once. Depending on your group, it could be better to introduce several rules at a time and add more over time. Too many rules at once can be overwhelming and feel like a dictatorship to the attendees—and if members of your organization feel oppressed or ignored, they won't come back!

Roles of meeting attendees

1. Leader

If you are the leader, you are in charge of planning the meeting from start to finish. A leader needs to decide to have a meeting, determine the best people to include for an effective meeting, and make sure everyone is prepared before the meeting begins.

2. Facilitator

Behind every great leader is a facilitator. The meeting facilitator should develop the agenda and establish ground rules before the meeting begins. Before the meeting, logistical information needs to be planned and any potential problems should be worked out. Some of the logistical items include when and where to have the meeting, what layout is best, whether you need refreshments, what to serve, and any materials and equipment needed.

3. Participants

You can lead a horse to water, but you can't make it sit down and participate in a boring meeting. Your attendees need to understand that you're holding a meeting for a reason and be able to participate. Do they understand the reason they are included and what is required of them?

Breaks

Donut jokes aside, should you really include refreshments and breaks in your agenda? Well, it depends on the length of the meeting. If the meeting will be less than an hour, a break is not usually needed. If the meeting is longer, you should schedule breaks about every hour or hour and a half. Bringing food or allowing a break for food allows meeting attendees to relax, enjoy themselves, and remain focused.[9]

Develop your agenda

If you are tired about hearing about agendas, let me repeat myself: A meeting without an agenda can be chaos. If you are the meeting leader and you decide not to use an agenda, these are some things that can happen:

- You will look unprepared and unprofessional

- Your group will be disorganized

9. Make sure you're not serving Thanksgiving dinner at your normal meeting or something. If you give participants too much food, they'll doze off!

- Your group may end up discussing the same thing at different meetings because you never seem to accomplish anything

- You may have an unusually high number of emergency meetings

- The Internet will shut off permanently, the global market will collapse, and the radios will only play polka music[10]

To see a sample agenda, flip to the back of the book and check out Appendix A.

Put it together

You know that the agenda needs to be prepared in advance and distributed to the attendees. It needs to be done at least one day before the meeting, but it would be much better if it was ready one week ahead. If you don't want to use an app or a program to create an agenda, you can make your own![11]

Fast Fact ───────────────────────

There have been 11 editions of "Robert's Rules of Order" since its original publication in 1876 (**www.robertsrules.com**).

10. Just kidding.
11. Reminder: See Appendix A for an example of an agenda.

CASE STUDY: DANIELLE HUTCHINS

Public Relations Specialist for
FreightCenter
dhutchins@freightcenter.com

When FreightCenter initiated its employee-led committee meetings for the first time, there were some concerns as to whether they would be effective. After all, we were asking our employees to take time out their busy work schedules to meet twice a month, and we didn't want to risk wasting their time. Whether your attendees are business professionals or students, their time is precious. Create an agenda and share it with your attendees before every meeting to avoid wasting time and to increase productivity. Doing this allowed me to successfully run meetings to plan for our biggest wellness event of the quarter: our first annual weight loss challenge: Drop It Like It's Hot 2016.

At the end of this case study is the agenda I used for my committee meetings. I'll go into more detail about the sections I've included, but first I want to talk about the importance of using an agenda and some tips on how to best utilize it.

The Importance of Using an Agenda

An unorganized meeting is stressful for everyone involved. It can lead to a loss of interest among your attendees, or, even worse, it can leave your attendees feeling frustrated or overloaded. The way your meeting is conducted will have a direct impact on its success and the best way to ensure a successful meeting is to plan ahead. That's where the agenda comes in. It's the best tool you'll find in planning and managing your meetings.

Agenda Tips

The following tips will help you create and use an agenda that works perfectly for your meetings.

- **Combine your agenda with your meeting minutes**: A good agenda provides an outline for the meeting that can used as a checklist to ensure that all information is covered. But, it's also the best place to write your meeting minutes. Combining the agenda and minutes as one document will help when it comes time to plan your next meeting.

- **Use a cloud-based service for easy sharing and group editing**: I use Google Docs for this, but you can use any web application that allows users to create and edit documents online while collaborating with other users in real time. This makes it easier to share your agenda with your attendees.

- **Share the agenda before the meeting**: This is important for two reasons: It helps your attendees prepare for the meeting so they can come equipped with any questions or information they'd like to propose, and it gives them a chance to recommend any items they think should be addressed, but aren't included.

- **Fill out the agenda**: It sounds simple, but filling out your agenda completely with detailed notes is crucial in ensuring that your meeting is effective. Make sure to include all the details you can before you send it out prior to the meeting and update it with your meeting minutes.

- **Share the agenda after the meeting**: We talked about the importance of sharing your agenda prior to the meeting. It's also a great idea to follow up with your attendees after the meeting by sharing the updated agenda.

Creating an Agenda Template

While the structure of your agenda template will rely heavily on the purpose of your meetings, there's a few details it should always include:

- **Meeting details**: The obvious — date, time and location.

- **Attendees**: Who do you expect to be at the meeting?

- **Old business**: Follow up with the action items from the last meeting.

- **New business**: What will you cover in this meeting?

- **Notes**: Use this section to take notes during your meeting.

- **Action items**: What must be done to complete your goals?

Here are a few sections I like to throw in:

- **Concerns**: It's a good idea to share concerns so they can be addressed effectively and in a timely fashion.

- **Praises/Shout outs**: I like ending my meeting on a positive note by shouting out employees who have done something great. At FreightCenter, we call them "Hi-5s."

- **Next week's agenda**: Let attendees know when the next meeting is and what they can expect it to cover.

Here is an example of an agenda from FreightCenter's health and wellness committee meetings. Check out the Google Docs version of the template here: **http://bit.ly/2asQ0KQ**. Want to use it? Upload it to your Google Drive and make a copy in order to edit the document.

WELLNESS COMMITTEE 04/18

04 MAY 2016 / 4:00 PM / MAIN CONFERENCE ROOM

ATTENDEES: DANIELLE H., JUSTIN R., RHIANNA D., CHRIS S., TERESA C.

AGENDA

Last Meeting Follow-up

- Goals decided upon for this quarter:

  - Get 100% of those employees who sign up for the Humana Vitality program registered for the Humana Vitality Check by May 14.

  - Get at least 30 people signed up to join a FreightCenter sponsored "Biggest Loser" type competition by May 14.

New Business

- Planning – Humana Vitality Check event

- Planning – Drop It Like It's Hot weight loss challenge 2016

NOTES

- Vitality Check

    - Training day Friday, 4/22 — five signed up so far

    - Still waiting on list of names. For now, let's promote by word of mouth.

    - Sending an email to management on Thursday, 4/21 to get their buy-in

    - Flyers posted around office (bathrooms, elevators, etc.)

- Drop It Like It's Hot

    - Email alert w/ signup will go out 5/2

    - Promotions: Internet page, flyers, word of mouth

    - Competition guidelines need to be written

CONCERNS

- This is the first time we've attempted a health and wellness initiative at FreightCenter. It will take a lot of planning and promoting to get people excited.

ACTION ITEMS

- Get the list of Vitality members (Danielle H.)

- Send an email to management (Rhianna D.)

- Create and post flyers (Justin R.)

- Write competition guidelines (Chris S.)

PRAISES, SHOUT-OUT'S, & HI-5'S

- Terese, Brandi, Felecia, and Alyssa already signed up for Humana Vitality and are racking up their rewards points!

- Teresa started a new work-out routine, Beach Body!

NEXT WEEK'S AGENDA

Review the competition guidelines and finalize plans for the Vitality check.

Danielle Hutchins is a young adult who leads bi-weekly wellness commit-tee meetings made up of employee volunteers. She started the committee to promote health and wellness throughout the company. She plans corpo-rate-sponsored wellness events and brainstorms ways to make a healthier and happier workplace.

Time-saving tips

Need to cut down the meeting time? Here are some suggestions to help you save those precious minutes and seconds.

- **Start Time**: This sounds like a no-brainer, but many meetings start late. Include the start time on your agenda.

- **Be Clear**: Make the instructions understandable, and, if necessary, write them down.

- **Pick Up the Pace**: Do not let the discussion grow stagnant. Keep things moving.

- **Prepare for Sluggishness**: Have a list of questions or possible topics prepared to get the creative juices flowing for tired groups.

ROBERT'S RULES QUICK REFERENCE:
How to Limit Debate

Why would I want to do this?

You think that some valid arguments are being made but too much time is being used, and you would like to offer a suggestion for a time limit.

- After being called on, you say, **"Madame/Mr. President, I move to limit discussion to one minute per speaker."**

Location and Room Layout

If you could choose anywhere to hold your meeting, where would you pick? A conference room in downtown Manhattan? A café in the middle of Paris? A dark cave with only a torch and some headlamps for light?

While you might not be able pick your ideal spot to hold a meeting, choosing the right room is important and will contribute to the effectiveness of the group. While you might stress over a way to choose a meeting room, the answer is simple: Decide how many people will attend your meeting. This will prevent a room that is too big or too small and will allow members of your group to feel comfortable.

Arrangement types

Believe it or not, the seating and table arrangement you choose make a big difference in the dynamics of your meeting. The type of layout depends on the size of the room, the number of attendees, the way the meeting will be conducted, and what you need to accomplish.

Circles and squares

This layout encourages all attendees to participate and interact with each other, but it requires you to decide whether to use tables. They are convenient if members need to write notes, but they can stop communication. That does not mean you cannot use tables; just be sure they are needed. This layout also shifts the focus away from the leader and onto all participants equally.

Semi-circles and U-shaped layouts

These layouts are good for problem solving, discussions, and meetings with attendee participation. Semi-circles and U-shaped room layouts are also good for meetings with visual aids. The meeting leader and visual aids can be placed at the "open" end of the room, because attendees will naturally look to the "front" of the setup.

Theatre style seating

In a meeting with many attendees, theatre style is ideal for arranging seats in parallel rows. Keep in mind that theatre seating is not conducive to discussions and interaction between the attendees. If you have to use a large auditorium but there are few attendees, have them sit in the center or in one section to create a team atmosphere.

Classroom seating

This style keeps your attendees facing forward and gives them a place to write or place materials on the table in front of them. This is not your best layout for meetings where you need participation, but you can use individual tables with three or four people at each to encourage them to work together as a group.

Preparing the space

You want to prepare the meeting space before the meeting begins. The appearance of the room makes a difference, especially if you have visitors. Use this checklist to see if your room is ready for your meeting!

1. Is your lighting sufficient?

    Yes   **No**

2. Is the room clean?

Yes   **No**

3. Is your equipment working?

Yes   **No**

4. Are there distracting noises of any kind?

Yes   **No**

5. Do you have a table to set up your giant donut buffet?

Yes   **No**

Create a friendly setting

A good meeting atmosphere is essential to a great meeting. Members of your organization should be relaxed and excited to be participating in your meeting. They should be free to move around if you're holding a longer meeting and feel comfortable speaking up if they need their voice to be heard. Put your attendees at ease, and survey them to make sure you are keeping them happy by the way you are running the meeting.

And always remember to . . .

Provide food if needed!!

Some people assume that you won't need food for every meeting, but I disagree. Throw caution to the wind! Provide a snack or let members of your organization bring their own. Hungry attendees = an unproductive and unfocused meeting.

Fast Fact

Hungry before the meeting? Eat an egg! Egg yolks contain lecithin, which helps you focus better, gain greater concentration, and improve memory recall (**www.inc.com**).

6

Effective Meeting Starters

You can engage or lose your audience in the opening minutes of any meeting. No matter if you're holding a meeting about Student Council, the Grammy Awards, or the Illuminati, it's important to get the audience's attention and show them that you are prepared.

Typical advice is to arrive at the meeting room 10 minutes early if you have things to set up, but you might want to get there 15 minutes early if not. This way, you can talk to people as they arrive and make them feel like part of the group.

Getting a Good Start

First, start on time. This is especially good when you meet with the same people on a regular basis. Your behavior will make it clear that you expect members of your organization to be ready on time.

Sometimes, people will be absent or late. In this case, you might need to rearrange the schedule to fit these problems. You'll also need to make a determination about how long to wait for latecomers.

Stuff happens. There will be instances when you personally will be unable to meet exactly on time. When this occurs, have a facilitator who can start the meeting until you arrive.

Warm up the group

Even an incredibly serious business meeting needs some social interaction. Whether you speak with members before the meeting or talk with them after, you need some socialization jump starts to warm them up and generate a team feeling:

- Getting everyone involved from the beginning

- Letting the attendees share their concerns or needs

- Breaking the ice for people who don't know each other

When you have attendees who don't know each other, a productive ice-breaker is to have each attendee share some personal information. You can use this example to help members feel part of the group and relaxed around others.

Name:

Year in School:

Why They Joined Your Organization:

Favorite Movie:

Favorite Flavor of Oreo™:

If there are only a few new people in attendance, many meeting leaders will only ask those people to introduce themselves. This is bad, because it makes the new attendees feel like outsiders and not members of the group.

Set the tone

Starting off with a friendly and group-oriented warm-up can set a great tone for the meeting. You have already asked each person to contribute something, which makes it easier for them to participate.

Remember: A productive and effective meeting requires work from the leader, the facilitator, the recorder, and every other person in attendance. The people in your organization are essential to making the meeting a success, and they need to contribute their thoughts and suggestions. Sharing information about themselves will create a sense of community.

At first, your group may need to review the ground rules at the beginning of each meeting, but don't feel tied to the rules if they aren't necessary. Certain rules may need to be reviewed from time to time, and the group may need to set aside time to review the rules periodically to see if changes are needed. If changes are needed, schedule time on the next agenda to talk about them.

Techniques to Use With Peers

Many group leaders want to jump right into the important business segment of the meeting, but sometimes, that isn't the best way to get things started. Easing attendees into the business element will bring attention to the meeting and draw them away from outside distractions. You can also explain how the meeting will be handled and remind members of your organization what will be expected during the meeting.

Call meeting to order

Active meetings can be busy, and sometimes you may have problems calling the group to "order." You need to call the meeting to order at the beginning, but you might need to do something similar after discussion periods on your agenda or after breaks. Here are some suggestions:

- Use a chime, bell, whistle, or any other noise maker

- Turn the lights off and back on

- Clap your hands

- Use a hand signal[12]

ROBERT'S RULES QUICK REFERENCE:
Guide to Rule Requirements

Charters	adopted by majority vote or as proved by law or authority, cannot be suspended
Bylaws	adopted by membership, cannot be suspended
Special Rules of Order	previous notice and two-thirds vote, or a majority, can be suspended by a two-thirds vote
Standing Rules	adopted with majority vote, can be suspended for session with a majority vote
Modified Roberts Rules of Order	adopted in bylaws, can be suspended with two-thirds vote

12. Be careful: This might not work with every group.

Get the group moving

Sometimes, it can be hard to get attendees involved in the meeting, and this is especially true early in the morning or right after school. If you need a few suggestions to keep members of your organization involved, you can use these ideas:

1. **Slow Breathing**

    Get the attendees to breathe slowly. It must be deep, cleansing breaths. Inhale deeply and exhale deeply. Bonus points if you can talk them into doing yoga and twisting themselves into human pretzels!

2. **Yawning Contest**

    Do you know who is the loudest yawner in your organization? Find out and organize a yawning contest!

3. **Dance-Off**

    Play some funky music and get your groove on! See who can do the "worm," the "dougie," or their best disco moves.

Games to Get Your Meeting Started

Sometimes a simple game can get things started and get the attendees to loosen up. Don't spend a lot of time playing games, but be sure to help members get to know each other. As you gain more experience, you can come up with ideas of your own. The important thing is to have fun and help members of your organization get acquainted and learn to work together. Always use methods to create a positive and friendly team atmosphere!

Bingo

This game is used to break the ice during a business meeting. Players need to fill up a horizontal, vertical, or diagonal line on the card. They do this by finding someone in the room that fits each requirement on the card. The details on the card can be personal or business related. When they find a person, have the person initial the card in one space and — bingo! Everyone has learned more about the other people in the meeting.

Break the Ice

This game gives you various ways to warm up your attendees and is especially good for people who are shy. You'll need name tags, felt markers, and index cards. Each attendee thinks of a nickname that describes him or her and then writes it on an index card and a stick-on nametag that should be turned face down. Collect the cards and read the nicknames aloud while the attendees try to guess who belongs to each nametag. When the person is identified, he or she can put the nametag on for all to see.

Dream Big

Break members into smaller groups and ask them to solve a ridiculous assignment. For example, you could ask members of your group to create the ultimate senior prank for the last day of school. After a few minutes, the groups will present the results to the whole group (and maybe you'll get some good ideas!).

Get to Know Each Other

Divide members into pairs. Some of the possible reasons to pair the two attendees can be that they've never met before, have different backgrounds, share the same hobbies, or are in different grades. Give the pairs a list of questions to discuss and get to know each other. Let them have some time alone. Give them a list of questions to discuss. These are some ideas, but you can use any questions to get them thinking.

- Why are you in this organization?

- What is your favorite/least favorite part of school?

- If you could go back to any time period, what would it be and why?

- Who would play you in a movie?

- What is your favorite animal?

- If you could only eat one food for the rest of your life, what would it be?

Group Résumé

This helps group members get acquainted and can help them see how their skills and experience complement each other. Divide attendees into groups of three to six members. Remind them that each member has experiences that should be acknowledged. Let them brag about their skills and use these details to create a résumé for the group. The attendees then create a résumé that represents the group as a team and presents it to the rest of the group. The résumé can include:

- Education

- Knowledge about your organization

- Years of experience

- Positions held

- Professional skills and experience

- Major accomplishments

- Hobbies and talents

In Sync

You need your meeting attendees to work together, and this game helps people learn to work with each other and have a team mentality. There are many different ways to do this, including the following:

- Challenge members to sing a simple song together.

- Have members develop a short story together. Each attendee adds one word.

- Pass a ball to the group and see how quickly they can pass it around without dropping it.

- Use LEGOs™ to build a project. Each person adds one or two pieces and sees what develops.

Quick Bits

Each person is given 30 seconds to tell others about themselves, their family, and their hobbies. Give the attendees an example of how this is done, and find a bell or buzzer to indicate their time is up.

Scavenger Hunt

This game helps attendees learn to work together to reach a common goal. To play, distribute five to ten statements and have attendees find someone who fits the description. Some examples include:

- Someone who likes pickles

- Someone who knows how to use a sewing machine

- Someone who has traveled outside the country

- Someone who plays soccer

- Someone who owns a snake

- Someone who has met a celebrity

Members need to take the statements and circulate around the room. They need to find people who fit each statement. When most of the answers are completed, collect the papers, and you can award a small prize to whoever has the most answers. Depending on your time frame, you can ask people about some of the most interesting things they learned.

Tell Us Who You Are

This is another way to help members get to know each other. Have all the participants write down two or three questions they would ask a person they just met. (It's way more fun if they are creative!) They should wander around the room and exchange questions and answers with others. It's more effective if they talk to people they don't already know. Give them five to ten minutes to gather information. Each attendee stands one at a time and has others tell the group what he or she just learned.

Fast Fact

A 2004 study showed that yawning was contagious in both chimps and humans (**www.newscientist.com**).

7

Running a Great Meeting

As the leader of your organization, you are important to the success of the meeting and keeping people focused on its purpose and goals. You need to make sure attendees' energy and attention stay on target.[13] But, how do you make sure your meeting is running smoothly?

To begin, let's analyze the three components of any meeting:

Meeting Components

1. Content

This includes attitudes, expectations, experience, ideas, knowledge, myths, and opinions shared by the participants. Remember that the content is not limited to the information that you present.

13. No pressure.

2. Participation

How do members of your organization interact with each other? Their feelings, attitudes, and expectations will have an impact on their willingness to cooperate, listen, and participate. Will the meeting have an "open" feeling?

3. Organization

This includes the way your agenda and information are organized to help you accomplish your goals for the meeting.

These three components are critical to maintaining an effective meeting, and a good leader keeps an eye on elements of each component. Successful and effective leaders can analyze what is happening and decide what action needs to be taken to keep the meeting on track. You want to gauge the progress being made and steer the attendees in the right direction.

Let's take a slightly deeper look into content, participation, and organization.

Content

1. Stay on Topic

The leader and participants of the meeting need to stay on topic. Keeping members of your group focused means that you'll be able to finish on time and accomplish your meeting goals.

2. Spur Participants to Action

When you need participants, the leader needs to encourage and generate participation from attendees.

3. **Evaluate All Points of View**

Your meeting becomes more effective when you note each point of view presented to the group.

4. **Plan of Action**

The group needs to develop a way to handle issues being discussed or problems that need solutions.

5. **Review**

A quick summary of topics can be valuable for members of your organization. Review the high points to make sure that all attendees understand what was discussed and any decisions that were finalized.

Participation

1. **Monitor**

Keep track of the people who participate and contribute to the meeting.

2. **Support**

Offer support for your attendees. This is especially important for people who need to contribute to the discussion but who may be shy or hesitant. Make sure they know that you are there to help!

3. **Encourage**

Be supportive to key people who offer their comments and details. You may need to ask quiet people to share their thoughts. One way to do this without undue pressure is to talk with them during a break and then call on them to speak.

4. **Difference of Opinion**

Any time you assemble a group of people, there will be differences and conflict. An effective leader can keep these potential disruptions to a minimum. However, some differences will help the group generate more possible solutions and thoughts for your agenda topics. Don't discourage useful differences, but be sure to maintain control of the situation. A truly effective leader can maintain control without being obvious about it.

5. Reactions

Watch the reactions of your attendees. How do various people react to the comments and suggestions? Can you use these reactions to your advantage? Sometimes, a person's reaction will give you an idea about who should work on various projects or which attendees would work well together.

6. Feedback

Feedback can work both ways. There are times when you need to offer feedback to attendees, and you should encourage the attendees to give their feedback about the meeting content, format, and execution. After they give feedback, the leader needs to evaluate it to make needed adjustments in the meetings. Refer to Chapter 12 for more advice on getting feedback.

Organization

1. Be Clear

Make the purpose and goals of the meeting clear. Attendees can be more helpful when they know what needs to be done.

2. Assign Roles

Each attendee needs to know what is expected of them. Some people will have more responsibilities, but each person needs to contribute something.

3. Time

It is critical to keep the meeting within the proposed time frame. This shows that you prepared thoroughly and are maintaining control of the meeting.

4. Have a Plan

The leader needs to develop a plan for presenting and distributing data, analyzing that data, finding options, sorting through feedback and suggestions, and making the final decisions.

5. Ground Rules

Review the ground rules occasionally to make sure they are effective, and change them if needed.

ROBERT'S RULES QUICK REFERENCE:
How to Suspend the Rules

This sounds cool, but why would I want to do this?

You would choose to suspend the rules if something you want brought up will seemingly not be discussed before adjournment.

- After being called on, you can say, **"Madame/Mr. Chairman, I move to suspend the rules and move item 8 to position 2."**

Quick notes:

Can I interrupt the speaker? **No.** Second needed? **Yes.** Debatable? **No.** Amendable? **No.**

Vote needed? **Two-thirds.**

Who Will Conduct the Meeting?

If you want someone else to be the leader of the meeting, you want to pick someone who will be able to:

- Call the meeting to order

- Understand the purpose and goals for the meeting

- Create the agenda and is familiar with the topics to be covered

- Pick the participants

- Lead the meeting

There are some cases where a meeting chair will be chosen based on whom the person knows, but this isn't the best way to pick the person who will control the meeting. A person should be chosen because of qualifications and experience. The leader has the greatest power to make a meeting succeed or mess it up, and when a leader is unprepared or unqualified, the meeting is a disaster.

This person needs to have the appropriate leadership skills. Self-confidence is an important trait for meeting leaders, but a large ego is not needed and can cause problems. Some of the key personality traits of an effective meeting chair include **objectivity, consideration, ethical behavior, and attitude.**

A leader who displays these qualities will build confidence in the attendees and lead to a successful meeting. A good leader will choose attendees with something to contribute, leading to a mutual respect and contributing to an effective meeting.

Maintaining control

Problems will crop up within any group of people, so the meeting leader needs to maintain control. There are times when he or she will be called on to resolve disputes. Here are some tips to help settle some of these situations.

The Scene: You're the leader of your chapter of Disco Music Fanatics at your high school. Robbie and Joanna are arguing about the best dance move of all time and look like they are about to start fist fighting! How do you resolve this conflict?

- Can you find mutual ground to bring the opposing people closer?

  "We're all passionate about disco music here!"

- Discuss possible ways to settle disagreements.

  "What if we have a dance-off to decide the best disco dance move?"

- Discuss the specific elements in dispute, avoid broad statements that are irrelevant to the issues being considered.

  "So Robbie thinks 'YMCA' is the best disco move, but Joanna is sure that the 'funky chicken' is the greatest dance of all time."

- Give each side an equal amount of time to voice their concerns.

  "You each have five minutes to discuss the pros and cons of the 'funky chicken' or the 'YMCA.'"

- When there is one side that is obviously right, steer the discussion that way.

  "Robbie is right—the 'funky chicken' and the 'YMCA' are both on a list of the Greatest Disco Moves of All Time."

- Find a way to state an individual opinion that highlights the best of both sides.

  "I think that both Robbie and Joanna have great points. Robbie is correct that the 'YMCA' is a really catchy song, and Joanna is right—everyone knows 'the funky chicken' is a hit at any disco party."

- When a debate is not going anywhere, end it.

  "How about we all just have a dance party instead?"[14]

Eliminating unnecessary distractions

Make sure to focus on legitimate business in your meetings. While it's fun (and often necessary) to talk about school, other organizations, or Taylor Swift's new album, you want to keep this at a minimum so you can finish the meeting in time.

---

14. A great way to end any conflict.

Fast Fact

The song "YMCA" by the Village People was released in 1978 (**www.huffingtonpost.com**).

ROBERT'S RULES QUICK REFERENCE:
How to Move to Recesss

Why would I want to do this?

You would choose to move to recess if debate has been going on for too long and you need a break.

- You can say, **"Madame/Mr. Moderator, I move to recess for an hour."**

Quick notes:

Can I interrupt the speaker? **No.** Second needed? **Yes.** Debatable? **No.** Amendable? **Yes.**

Vote needed? **Majority.**

Effectively Manage the Meeting

Most people are aware that many ineffective meetings are held every day because their leaders are unacquainted with meeting skills or are unprepared. Here is an example of something you should never do:

The meeting is scheduled to begin at 10 a.m., but the leader of Disco Music Fanatics, Jo King, is not there. Minutes click by, but Jo doesn't show up. No one in attendance has any idea where Jo is or when she will arrive. Eventually, at 10:20 a.m., Jo rushes in the door with a big pile of papers. She lays the papers on the table and simply says, "We need to get busy. There is a lot of work to do today."

I have been in meetings that began like this with no apology and rude, unprofessional behavior. If you will be late, call to let attendees know when you will be there. Otherwise, the meeting starts on a negative note.

The Facilitator

While it sounds like a cool new professional wrestler, a facilitator is actually a vital member of your meeting. The facilitator handles the details of the meeting so that the leader can get more involved in the discussion and problem-solving elements without having to worry about the details of handling a meeting. If you have enough qualified people, a separate leader and facilitator make for a better quality meeting. However, the leader is ultimately responsible for the outcome of the meeting even if there is a facilitator.

Remember, the meeting leader and facilitator are not the same position. It is much better to have two different people handle these roles. Many leaders have a specific interest in the meeting goals, and this makes it impossible or difficult for them to remain neutral when discussing problems or situations.

Too much control

Facilitators need to be careful not to smother the meeting. Experienced leaders know the right times to let the group talk freely and when to exert more control. It is a fine line, but it can be learned with practice. These are some signs that the facilitator is using too much control.

- The leader or facilitator talks too much

  "I will now be discussing 35 of my favorite disco moves, starting with 'the Hustle.'"

- Too little participation from the other attendees

  "Does anyone know 2+2? Anyone? Anyone?"

- The leader is bossy, overly confident, and pushy

  "I am definitely the best disco dancer in this entire school . . . and probably the world!"

- The leader is overly aggressive and domineering

  "On your knees, peasants!"

Really, why would I want to do this?

You would do so if you disagree with a decision the chairperson has made.

- Without recognition, you say, **"I appeal from the decision of the chair."**

Quick notes:

Can I interrupt the speaker? **Yes.** Second needed? **Yes.** Debatable? **Yes.** Amendable? **No.**

Vote needed? **Majority.**

Exhibiting any of these traits is not in the best interest of the meeting. Each attendee should be there for a reason and each needs to participate. This is especially critical in problem-solving meetings.

Facilitators should not micromanage meetings. If the agenda is prepared properly and the attendees are given time to prepare, there should not be any reason to micromanage the meeting or the group. Have you noticed how attendees of some meetings seem to tune out things when they are being controlled too much? They feel manipulated or useless, and no one responds well in these situations.

Train group members to facilitate

Facilitating a meeting is not some mysterious secret that only a Yoda-like creature would know. If you are in an organization that has periodic or frequent meetings, you should have a number of people trained to facilitate. Here are some of the skills any meeting facilitator should possess.

- Keep the group members involved.

- Have high energy and enthusiasm.

- Listen well, and bring the meeting back to the main subject when it drifts off course.

- Encourage all attendees to participate without putting them on the spot or making them feel uncomfortable.

- When attendees are disruptive, the facilitator needs to take control of the situation.

- Be alert to attendees who have a hidden agenda, and squelch this behavior.

- Keep a sense of humor and learn to use it effectively in the meeting.

- Pay special attention to concerns or needs of the newest group members.

- Remain objective—this helps to keep the discussion on track and encourages attendees to share differing viewpoints and thoughts.

- Be forceful when needed, but do not be harsh. Know when to interrupt and when to stand back and let the attendees discuss issues.

- No matter what happens, the facilitator must do what is needed to see the meeting reaches its goals.

- It is important to create an atmosphere where the attendees feel safe, so that they can be comfortable expressing their creative side.

Facilitator skills

There are also certain specific skills that can help build your group and make the attendees stronger. A few of these skills include:

- **Being Clear:** You might need to elaborate on ideas and suggestions to make sure all attendees understand the details.

- **Understanding Moods**: Every group of people will have a certain mood. The facilitator needs to learn to gauge the mood and take action to improve the mood when needed.

- **Being Positive**: Remember to be encouraging and respond promptly to concerns and questions.

- **Watching:** Watch the attendees for potential problems, and take breaks as needed. If someone is about to faint from hunger, it might be a good idea to take a five-minute donut break.

- **Work Together**: Groups need someone to be a mediator to help them explore their differences and concerns. Most differences can be worked out; it just takes patience and a clear head.

Who should train facilitators?

Look for someone in the group who has facilitating experience. If so, that person could be your first choice. It would be good to become familiar with his or her facilitating skills before you ask the person to train other people.

Any time you have a new person facilitating, it is best to inform the group and ask them to be patient, helpful, and understanding. The facilitator will get better with practice. During any practice, someone needs to be assigned to take notes of things the facilitator needs to work on. These notes should include good points and bad points. Right after the meeting, this person should speak with the facilitator trainee to review the things they need to practice.

Leadership Skills

It's true that effective leadership will set the tone for any organization. Some people are progressive thinkers, aren't afraid of public speaking, and can easily create a good working environment. If you're more on the shy side, don't worry — leadership skills develop with experience.

People in leadership roles have to show confidence and understand all information necessary for their meetings and organization. Communication is important. Make sure to meet with your organization's advisor to talk about current issues and the agendas you want to set for your group. Decisions become a lot clearer when everyone inside and outside of the organization knows how and why they were made.

ROBERT'S RULES QUICK REFERENCE:
How the Chair Announces Results

The chair may say one of two things when a motion is voted on:

- **"The ayes have it,"** which means the motion carries and the chair will detail the effect of the vote.

- **"The nays have it,"** which means that the motion failed — better luck next time!

CASE STUDY: DAVID REISS

Professor of Law
Academic Program Director, Center
for Urban Business Entrepreneurship
Brooklyn Law School

I teach a Community Development Clinic where I instruct my students on how Robert's Rules of Order can help not-for-profit organizations achieve their goals. I have also sat on community boards and not-for-profit boards and have relied on Robert's Rules of Order myself on many occasions.

If I had one takeaway from my experience, it is that you, as the leader, should work as hard as possible to minimize personality conflict when the path is smooth so that things don't get out of hand when you begin facing a rocky road ahead. This means providing a good example for others to set an appropriate tone for meetings. It means avoiding "ad hominems" — attacks on people themselves, not their ideas. It means calling people out when they cross the line in the meeting so that people are reminded that they should monitor their own behavior.

I have been present at community board meetings where an evenly keeled Chair is able to maintain order in the face of very angry and/or slightly crazy attendees. I have also seen Chairs who are able to maintain order when the body is deeply divided on issues of great importance to the members. With a good Chair, it is very rare for the meeting to get out of hand; with a bad Chair, it can be commonplace (and very annoying).

If you, as the leader of the meeting, always keep the purpose of the organization or club at the front and center of your agenda, you should be able to set a tone that the work is primarily about your shared goals and not about the personalities in the room.

*David Reiss is a professor of law at Brooklyn Law School. He teaches a Community Development Clinic there and spends part of his time teaching students about Robert's Rules of Order, because they represent not-for-profit organizations. He has also sat on community boards and not-for-profit boards. Visit his blog at **http://refinblog.com**.*

Look like a leader

If you have the communication skills of a leader, but are worried about your appearance, here are some skills you can use to ensure you really look like a leader.

Dress for success

The way we look does make a difference in how we feel. It also affects how we project ourselves to others. People respond positively to people who appear self-assured and enthusiastic. This means that it's important for you to analyze the way you look so you can dress for success.

Here are some tips to create your meeting outfits:

- Use color in your wardrobe. Bold colors have a different effect than muted colors. Black, dark blue, gray, tan, brown, and similar colors can blend in with the background. However, red, green, blue, yellow and other bright colors will make you stand out. Although bright colors are not all you need, they will help to instill excitement in your attendees and prepare them for the information to be shared. An easy and inexpensive way to accomplish this is as easy as adding a colorful scarf or other accessory to spice up your wardrobe.

- You should not dress too casually or in loose fitting clothes. Each of these things will give you a relaxed appearance, but will also make you seem unprofessional.

- If you're leading a Very Important Meeting, wear pressed clothes, crisp collars and seams. You want to wear clothes that fit well, present a professional image, and make the attendees see you as a leader.

If you are still unsure about what to wear for a meeting, just wear whatever makes you feel confident and professional. Do you feel more at home in high heels and a blazer or a three-piece suit and tie? A t-shirt and jeans? What about a faux-fur coat and a bright red wig? Wearing uncomfortable clothing that makes you feel silly and nervous won't help you effectively lead others. Remember, the key is to be confident and excited to start your meeting!

Body language

Your body language conveys a lot of information to meeting attendees. Walk into the room with your head high and back straight, and you will instill confidence, showing that you are in charge. If you walk into a meeting with your head hanging low and you look timid, the meeting will get away from you. When in doubt, you can look at this chart, found in the book "Running a Meeting That Works, Third Edition" by Robert F. Miller and Marilyn Pincus.

P – Posture—upright, not sagging. Capable.

O – Obviously caring. Smiling, listening. Involved.

W – Walk tall. Do not drag your feet or slouch shoulders. Secure.

E – Eye contact. Direct. Intent.

R – Relaxed body, especially arms, hands, shoulders. Calm.

Fast Fact

93% of all communication is nonverbal (**www.lifesize.com**).

8

How to Tell if Your Meeting Is Awesome

Good news! You've planned and executed your first meeting, and no one cried, screamed, or threw chairs out of the windows. You're feeling pretty confident about your skills as a leader and about the participants of your meeting. But how can you tell if your meeting is truly awesome?

Your Attendees Are Motivated

Motivation is critical to maintaining morale and participation. Unmotivated employees who dread attending meetings and have bad attitudes from the time they arrive until they leave are unpleasant for everyone to deal with.

Motivated attendees work harder to help the group reach its goals, improving the situation for everyone in the meeting. A pleasant, hard-working organization makes your job easier.

Creating and keeping positive attitudes

Attitudes influence how people feel about any task or topic and can stifle their participation. These conditions can affect a participant's attitude.

- **Their feelings and thoughts about something affect their reaction.** When they think good things, they will feel positive. When they tell themselves bad things, they will have a negative attitude. This gives them the power to feel good or bad about something.

- **Their state of mind has an impact**. It is affected by what they tell themselves.

  How do they react to their own feelings?

A positive attitude improves the morale of your attendees. Have you been in a meeting with a miserably unhappy person? Even if the meeting for Busybodies Anonymous Club is going well, if Jerry is acting like a jerk, the entire meeting can go downhill. Find ways to motivate your team and avoid negativity. Negative, hurtful, and defensive thoughts cause bad attitudes and limit productivity. Attitudes are contagious. Be enthusiastic about the tasks before the group.

Another thing that promotes positive attitudes is showing an interest in members of your organization and about the group's success. There are simple things you can do that mean a lot to them and prove that you realize they are human beings with lives outside of school. Recognize their birthdays, other interests, pets, favorite kinds of ice cream, or anything else that involves their personal lives.

Motivation prompts productivity

Your group will thrive in your meetings when you have a productive team taking the pressure off you and making it easier to plan for a good meeting.

Here are some tips to increase their productivity in your group:

- Your group will face problems from time to time. Encourage your attendees to offer solutions. They could offer ideas you can use or they might not. Either way, they are involved in solving the problem. Show that you value their thoughts and opinions.

- Have competitions between the members of your organization to find solutions, but do not pit people against each other in a negative way.

- Look for ways to make the group's duties easier. These ideas may be new ways to do things or may improve on your current procedures to achieve productivity, because the duties will be handled faster and smoother.

- Teach your attendees to understand the importance of productivity.

Avoid favoritism

Showing favoritism can cause problems in your meetings. Playing favorites will "unmotivate" your attendees.[15] As the meeting leader, you need to take the time and make the effort to motivate your staff. Showing favoritism will undo your efforts.

Some favoritism with attendees may not be a big deal, but it has negative repercussions. If you only call on your best friend or your significant other in the meeting, the attitude of your meeting attendees might not be so favorable.

Favoritism can occasionally be a good thing. You should recognize others for their hard work, but you also need to be able to justify your favoritism. If you cannot justify it to yourself, there is no chance that members of your organization will believe you.

Recognizing participants for excelling at their tasks can motivate them to continue to do well and motivate others to work harder.

Encourage improvement

Everybody likes to see people in his or her group or team making improvement. Attendee improvement means better productivity. You can encourage attendees to improve by motivating them. Most people want to do better, and your encouragement will help them.

People try to do better when someone supports them. Show support for your meeting participants, and let them know you are available when they

15. That is not a real word.

have problems. This can motivate them to take chances and can help them improve. As they improve, they become more valuable in your meetings.

Say a member of Disco Music Fanatics comes up to you and asks a question about the history of a dance move you've never heard of before: the "Parliamentary Procedure."[16] How do you handle it? Would you help him or her learn more about this crazy dance move or shrug it off and ignore the person?

When members come to you about a task, it is usually because they want to improve. Remember they can become bored when you do not challenge them and encourage them to do more. Your offer to help them improve is motivating and helps them become more enthusiastic about your organization. They want to do more and strive for more responsibility.

ROBERT'S RULES QUICK REFERENCE:
How to Amend a Motion

What does it mean to amend a motion?

Amending a motion means that you want to change some sort of wording or detail.

- After the chair calls on you, you say a variation of the following:

  "Madame/Mr. Chairman, I move that the motion be amended by adding the following words . . ."

  "Madame/Mr. Chairman, I move that the motion be amended by striking the following words . . ."

---

16. That is not a real dance move.

"Madame/Mr. Chairman, I move that the motion be amended by striking the following words and adding . . . in their place."

Quick notes:

Can I interrupt the speaker? **No.** Second needed? **Yes.**
Debatable? **Yes.** Amendable? **Yes.**

Vote needed? **Majority.**

It's important that you remember to praise members of your organization. The best participants will get tired of being taken for granted. Tell meeting attendees on a regular basis that you appreciate them so that they will continue to do a consistent and superior job. People never get tired of being praised. If they do an amazing job at five consecutive meetings, tell them you appreciate that effort each day. It takes little effort to say "thank you"

and "good job," but you will be rewarded by happy and motivated members of your organization.

> ## Fast Fact
>
> According to Robert's Rules, a quorum is the minimum number of voting members who must be present at a properly called meeting in order to conduct business in the name of the group. A quorum should consist of "as large as can be depended upon for being present at all meetings when the weather is not exceptionally bad" (**www.dummies.com**).

Games to motivate

Compliments!

This is an exercise that helps people learn how to give positive feedback to others. To play, pair up members of your group and ask each participant to find something positive about his or her partner, and then share that with the group.

A Little Better

Have volunteers stretch their arms as high as possible on the wall. Find some way to mark how far they reach. Have them stretch their arms again even higher. Mark the new spots they reach. Believe it or not, it is almost always higher than the first marks. If they don't reach higher, encourage them more. Ask the attendees for their conclusions, and follow up the exercise with a few questions, such as: "Is there anything I could do to improve this organization?" and "Are there ways you could help improve this organization?"

My Idea of Success Is . . .

This quick exercise is a way to help people see how their values and the values of others change as their situations and experience change. Remind the attendees that our idea of "success" is highly individualized, ask two or three people what their idea of success is, and then ask the following questions:

- When you were in elementary school, what was your idea of success?

- What made a person a success in your eyes at that time?

- How did you define success now?

- Do you see yourself as a success? Why or why not?

Good Team Atmosphere

If your group works well together and solves problems easily, you're running a good meeting. However, sometimes, members of an organization don't have a lot in common and have a hard time bonding and forming a team. A great example of this is the classic '90s movie "The Mighty Ducks 2." The Ducks needed to trust each other so they could win the global hockey championship against Iceland. Here are some games you can play so you too can chant the phrase "Ducks Fly Together!" without a shred of irony.

What's on This Penny?

This game demonstrates the importance of working together as a team and that each person has something to contribute to the project. You need a handout that shows both sides of a coin and another handout that only contains two circles. On one of which, write "Front of a Penny," and, on the other, "Back of a Penny."

- Have each person take a few minutes to list each feature of a penny from memory.

- You can have each person list how many things he or she got correct.

- Have the attendees work together with their lists and give them a few minutes to see if they found everything.

- Recalculate and find how many items each team got correct.

- The differences illustrate what can be accomplished by working as a team.

ROBERT'S RULES QUICK REFERENCE:
How a Motion is Voted On

- The chair says: **"Are you ready for the question?"**

  If you want to debate or speak on the motion, claim the floor now!

- If no one rises, a vote is taken

- The chair then says: **"The question is on the adoption of the motion that . . . As many as are in favor, say 'Aye.'** (Waits for response.) **Those opposed say 'Nay.'** (Waits for response.) **Those abstained please say 'Aye.'"**

  What does abstained mean?

  Abstained means those who do not wish to cast a vote

What Is Your Claim to Fame?

This activity encourages attendees to share personal information with each other. Decide on one provocative question that you will ask at each meeting. You can include the question on the agenda or just wait until the meeting begins. Each participant needs to write an answer in 20-30 words and share with the group. Some sample questions could include:

- What possession do you treasure the most?

- Whom do you admire? Why?

- What is the best book you ever read? Why is it the best?

- What is your hidden talent?

- What is your favorite joke?

Traits of a Leader

This exercise helps the traits and qualities a leader needs. Have attendees list five people who they consider to be leaders.[17] Then, divide the attendees into groups and have them compare lists. Why did they choose those particular leaders? What qualities do all of their choices have in common?

Fast Fact ═══════════════════════════════

The most current copy of *Robert's Rules* was published in 2011.

---

17. My personal five are Michelle Obama, Freddie Mercury, Mafia mob boss Al Capone, Lizzy McGuire, and Ms. Frizzle from "The Magic School Bus."

Effective Listening

Listening is a big part of communication. There are verbal and nonverbal listening skills, and both of these are important for effective facilitation and leadership during a meeting. Remember that both techniques have their place in your meetings.

Verbal listening

Verbal listening skills include reviewing the information that has been shared with the group. This can include summarizing details the speaker or other attendees said to the meeting attendees. These are listening skills to help you be a better, more effective leader or facilitator. When someone says they are tired of the way things are, these are a few ways you can reply.

- "So, you are tired of the way the meeting is run?"

- "Are you saying that you want to recommend some changes?"

- "You sound irritated and unhappy with our meeting."

- "Will you tell me what you don't like about our meeting?"

Each reply accomplishes something different, and the one you use depends on the person you are talking with and what you need to accomplish with them.

Nonverbal listening

Nonverbal listening includes a different set of skills. Check each of these categories in order to fully understand what members of your meeting aren't saying out loud.

Body Position

You want to look equal when you're talking to other members of your group, so you want to think about your body position. To convey equality, try sitting on the edge of a table or chair. Maintain a relaxed position for equal feelings. Never crowd the person or get in his or her face.

Facial Expressions

Your facial expressions can affect the person you are listening to. Don't yawn, look bored, or roll your eyes, and remember to smile at the right times. Your face reveals a lot about what you are thinking and feeling.

Silence

People need time to express themselves, and many times, they need the person to just stay quiet for a few minutes. Give them time to form the words to get their point across to you and the other attendees.

Learn to Ask Questions—The Right Way

If you shout a question at members of your organization, it is likely they will shout the answer back at you. On the other hand, if you sound calm and pleasant, attendees are likely to respond in a positive manner. Avoid tones or words that seem adversarial or confrontational.

Effective leaders need to communicate with attendees effectively. Take time to discover what you want to know—think of it like planning a trip. You know where you want to end up at the Grand Canyon, but you need to figure out how to get there. Will you take a car, plane, or ride horseback? If you begin that trek with no plan, you won't get very far. In the same vein, you may wander around with useless questions in your meeting before you reach the answer you and the group need.

Types of questions

Some questions will clarify your point, while others expand your understanding of facts or issues. The questions you should use depend on what you want to learn. Do you need a simple answer or a more complicated and involved answer? The explanations below will help you understand how to phrase questions to draw out the answers you need.

- **Clarification and Confirmation**: Begin your questions with: "Can," "Do," "Is," "Will," "When," "Who," and "Did." These questions will lead to yes or no answers or other short answers. Use these questions when you do not need a lot of details. These are called "closed" questions.

- **Additional Clarification**: Begin these questions with "How," "What," and "Why." The answers to these questions need more detailed answers. They are called "open" questions because they require more thought and effort, and they give you more information.

- **Expand the Response**: Answers to these questions let you dig deeper for details. Use these questions after you get partial answers to your other questions. Those initial answers will help you know what other information is needed.

The better your questions become, the more comfortable and responsive the meeting attendees should be with you. Make them feel comfortable, and you should gain more useful information. They will hold back when they are uncomfortable.

Fast Fact

A "proxy" is when a member who expects to be absent from a meeting authorizes someone else to act in his or her place at the meeting (**www.robertsrules.com**).

9

Tools for Making Your
Meeting Great

Your organization is working as a team, and you're proud of your people skills thus far. But what about your actual *tools* needed to run an effective meeting?

Here are some questions to consider to determine the best way to organize and gather the information you plan to use in your meeting.

1. Do you have the information that you need?

   Yes   **No**

2. Is there enough information for a thorough presentation?

   Yes   **No**

3. Are all elements of the topic or subject represented in the information you have?

   Yes   **No**

4. Do you need additional people to help you collect more information?

   Yes   **No**

5. Have you organized the information you plan to present?

   Yes   **No**

6. Can your group use the information the way you have it organized?

   Yes   **No**

7. Is further organization needed?

   Yes   **No**

Prepare Data

Before you start your meeting, you need to prepare the information, or data, you will be communicating to the group. The steps involved in preparing the data include gathering, organizing, grouping, sequencing, and breaking it down.

Gather

There are a lot of different ways to gather information. Below, you will find more details on some of these methods.

ROBERT'S RULES QUICK REFERENCE:
How to Move to a Committee of the Whole

What? Why would I want to do this?

You would choose to move to a committee of the whole if you are planning to propose something controversial and would like to limit the potential of it being killed, the press being around, or other random visitors.

- After being called on, you say, **"Madame/Mr. Chairman, I move that we go to a committee of the whole."**

Brainstorming

Brainstorming allows the group to get all ideas out in the open and to share thoughts about these ideas. Someone needs to be assigned to document all ideas that arise. Encourage everyone involved to be creative and open-minded. It is important to keep the group focused on the topics that need to be discussed.

The best way to brainstorm is to:

- Explain the situation or problem.

- Make the goals known to all participants.

- Make brief notes about all elements and ideas that are discussed.

- Review and redefine your list during the brainstorming session.

- Set a plan of action in motion.

Surveys and Questionnaires

Surveys and questionnaires are another way to gather information. It is an obvious way to find out what people think about any topic. A good survey or questionnaire can reveal useful information that you can use. Be sure that you do not talk over the heads of people. Make it easy to understand.

When you ask questions, make the problem clear and tell participants what you need to accomplish. Present the questions to attendees and keep the questionnaire less than 25 questions. When you have the completed surveys, compile the results to see what you have learned.

Interviews

Interviews can be a great way to gather information. When you interview someone, it is important to explain why you need to speak with him or her. Outline the problem or area that you need information about. What do you hope to accomplish with the interview? The questions should be prepared ahead of time and in such a way that they generate the information that is needed. Set a specific time to meet with the person or people.

When you speak to the person or people, they need to know some specific information.

- Who you are and why you need to speak with them.

- Tell them the reason for the interview—the goal and purpose.

- Tell them why the information is important and why you feel they can help.

- If the meeting is confidential, let them know.

- Explain why you chose them and what they can contribute.

- Be clear about how the information will be used and about any follow-ups.

Organize

After you collect data, you need to organize it in some manner. Otherwise, the information is useless.

T-Charts

A T-chart is the familiar "pro and con" list that can be used to compare information. Some of these things may include:

- Pro vs. Con

- Start vs. Stop

- Behavior or Action compared to Benefits

- Old vs. New

These are only some of the possibilities. A T-chart can also have three columns. Three-column charts are called Double T-Charts. Use either of these to evaluate the information you collected.

When you create a T-Chart, define the problem to be addressed and the goals you hope to reach. Draw a T-shaped frame and insert a header over the chart and headers for each column to keep the information organized. Insert each piece of information in the appropriate column. Continue until all items are entered in one column. The meeting attendees can then review the chart and analyze the information to form a plan of action.

Matrix Charts

Matrix Charts are a common way to organize information. They help the group find a plan of action, make choices about the direction to be taken, keep different issues separated, evaluate the information and chart these details in a way that others can review and understand the information. See the example below.

	Meeting Preparation	Meeting Agenda	Meeting Room Setup & Food	Meeting Room Cleanup
Kim	X			X
Khloe		X	X	
Kendall		X		X
Kylie	X		X	

Display it

There are times when you need to display the information that you gathered. You can do this through area graphs, bar graphs, line graphs, a pie chart,[18] or any other way that may be convenient for you and your group.

ROBERT'S RULES QUICK REFERENCE:
How a Motion Will Be Considered

- Members are allowed to debate the motion

- Members must get permission to have the floor from the chair while debating, with one person speaking at a time

- The member responsible for the motion may speak first

- Debate must deal only with the motion being discussed

- Debate ends when two-thirds of the assembly votes for closure or by order of the chair if no one wants to debate further

18. Cherry, peach, or apple are my favorites.

Selected Tools

You can use many different kinds of tools when executing your meeting, but each situation calls for a different tool. This information should help you determine which tools are right for your particular meeting.

Paper

Ah, paper — a classic choice. Use it to organize or display information for your group. It works well when you are brainstorming and problem solving and is great for timelines. Butcher paper is especially easy to use and gives you a large area for notes and additions. A long piece of paper gives all attendees a chance to participate and share their thoughts.

Chalkboard

A chalkboard can be placed on an easel, a stand, or mounted on the wall. It's an easy way to make notes and display specific information. Chalkboards and white boards are best for groups of fewer than 25 people in an informal setting because the information can be changed if needed. Make sure someone is keeping written notes on paper for later reference—this gives you a permanent record of the information while allowing you to make changes on the board for the group.

Smart Board

A Smart Board, if you have one, is easy to use and very helpful for meetings. It is an interactive whiteboard that allows people to "write." They are a great way to show information because it can be displayed in a large group of people. However, you might want to have a permanent record of the information when you're using a Smart Board in case your data is erased.

Overhead Projector or Computer

Want to go old school? Use a projector. Clear sheets (usually acetate) are used with overhead projectors. They can be a good way to present information to a group without the computer requirements needed for a PowerPoint presentation. You can easily make notes on the sheets with a felt tip marker.

However, if you'd rather be up-to-date in the 21st century, you can always use a computer in order to display information. A PowerPoint presentation or a Prezi normally gets the message across pretty well. This tool is useful for groups of 20-75 people but depends on the layout of the room.

ROBERT'S RULES QUICK REFERENCE:
How to Refer to a Committee

Why would I want to do this?

You would choose to refer to a committee if you feel that an idea needs more study or input.

- After you have been called on, you would say, **"Madame/ Mr. Chairman, I move that the question be referred to a committee made up of members Charles, White, and Stewart."**

Props

There are a number of props you can use in your meetings, including visual aids, nametags, and basic supplies. Below are some props that can be used to add some flavor to your meeting, spurring some more creative, entertaining ideas. If you know your attendees, you should be able to gauge whether these ideas will be well received.

- Caps or hats

- Posters or signs

- Gifts

- A cardboard cutout of Edward from "Twilight"

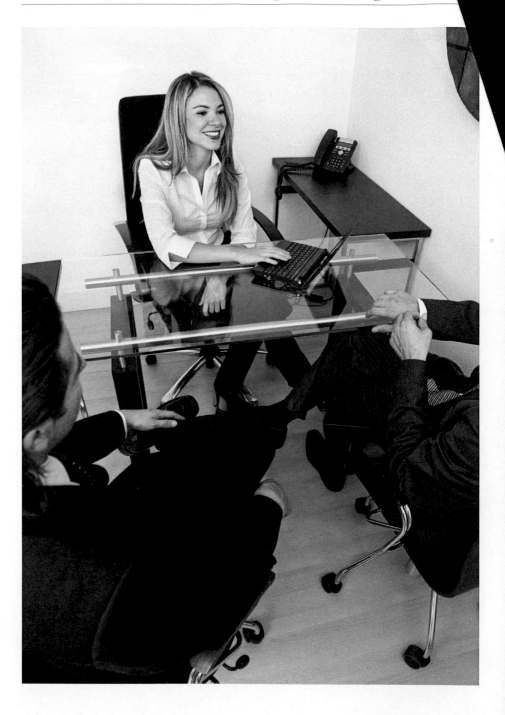

...ntations

...would you define your presentation style? Do you recite facts and ...istics in a monotone voice? Do you use a T-shirt cannon to excite meet-.ng attendees? Or do you present confidently with an informative, interesting display on a PowerPoint?

Many presentations aren't well prepared or delivered, which means that they are often dreaded during a meeting. However, there are three essential components to creating an interesting, well-thought-out presentation.

The audience

The first step in creating an effective presentation is to get to know your attendees. It's important that you know the people who will hear your presentation to convey the information well. Ask yourself the following questions.

- Who will be in the audience?
- What sort of people are they?
- What do they need and expect from you?
- What do they need and expect from this presentation?

These questions will help you get started with your presentation. You have expectations for the presentation, but so do the attendees. The questions will also help you to tailor the information for the attendees to present the details they need and to avoid duplicating things they already know.

Prepare your presentation

Your presentation needs to communicate good information to the attendees. Some of the information will need to overlap to move from one point to another and to tie it together. First, determine the main points that you want and need to convey. Don't try to cover too much information in a presentation or you will feel overwhelmed.

Handouts can be helpful for your attendees, but keep them simple and short. They can be sent out before the meeting with the agenda or after the meeting. When you distribute handouts during the meeting, attendees can be absorbed in reading these and may not pay attention to your presentation.

When to accept questions

Questions can be asked at the beginning, the middle, or the end of your presentation. Here are some ways to determine when questions would be most appropriate.

Beginning

Questions at the beginning require that the attendees be familiar with the topic. This is the best way for them to ask intelligent and specific questions. Questions at the start will help you know what the attendees are thinking. It's also good for you to have a broad knowledge of the topic to make alterations in order to accommodate the questions posed.

During

Questions during the meeting are better for small, informal groups. You can say that the participants should feel free to ask questions during your presentation. This is a great way to keep the group involved in the presentation, but be warned: Questions can get out of hand.

After

The most common time to answer questions is at the end of the presentation to avoid interruptions. At this point, the attendees can ask more informed questions. Your presentation should have answered many of their questions and limit the number that need to be addressed by the end. Announce that you are finished and ask for questions.

Fast Fact —————————————————

PowerPoint was first created in 1987, but officially launched in 1990.

10

Problem Solving

What if Dave "The Big Squeeze" Johnson never shows up to help decorate the homecoming float? Or Dina Soars keeps falling asleep? Or Hazel Nutt *Will. Not. Shut. Up.* when you're trying to talk? How would you handle these difficulties? No matter how well you run your meeting, there will be always problems from time to time, but it's important to remember that they are "people problems" and can be resolved.

Solving the Problem

What factors drive "people problems?" Egos, likes, dislikes, insecurities, ambitions, moods, and a wide variety of personalities. Bigger problems happen when others in the group react to the people causing the initial issue.

Let's say you're the *very* enthusiastic president of the Dynamic Digeridoos, your school's Digeridoo choir. The spring concert, themed "Whale Noises," is quickly approaching, but barely anybody has shown up to rehearsal. How do you solve this problem?

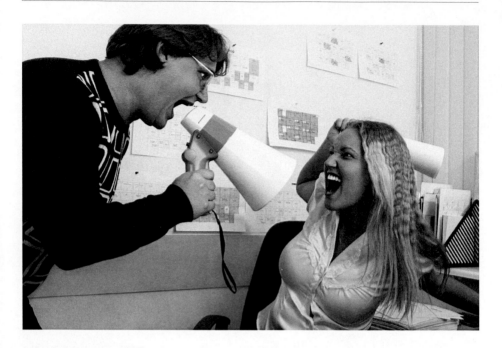

Figure out the cause

These are the most common situations that cause conflict to escalate.

Miscommunication

Many people do not listen to each other, failing to understand what is being said.

> *"I thought you said rehearsal was on Monday, not Thursday!"*

Observation

Two different people can see the same thing in different ways. This can be even worse when there are multiple people in the group who see the situation differently.

> *"I know you're really invested in Digeridoos, but I don't think we need to practice at all."*

Preferred Developments

Different people can want various things to happen when a situation is resolved or a problem is solved.

"I hate this theme, and I hate this music!"

Values

People decide what they feel is acceptable or proper based on their personal values, which may vary greatly.

"I can't believe you called me at 3 a.m. to see if I would come into rehearsal the next morning! That's totally unacceptable."

Understand the conflict

If the meeting leader understands the conflict, it's easier to manage. The way you deal with conflict has a major impact on the attendees and the overall success of your meeting. It can also affect how participants deal with each other in future meetings. There are four basic ways to approach this problem. The situation will dictate which approach should be used in each situation.

Avoidance

Some conflicts do not need to be resolved right away. When it is trivial, there is no reason to make the situation worse. It's a good idea to watch the situation and see if more involvement is needed.

"Maybe I'll cancel the concert and bring it up later."

Strike a Bargain

This is a good way to compromise when an ideal solution is not possible. It works well when each side is willing to give a little. Let them decide what they are willing to give up and what they feel is nonnegotiable, and start there. Usually, each party can make some concessions while retaining particular concerns.

"Why don't we have the rehearsal at 3:30 p.m. after school instead of 6 a.m.?

Make Demands

People who approach conflict by demanding their way are self-centered. There will be a winner and a loser. Meeting leaders need to head off situations that will divide the group.

"I demand all of you apologize to me immediately!"

Solve Problems

This approach can maintain the relationship along with winning. The people involved work together to find a solution that works for each of them. Finding the solution is only the first step—there needs to be a creative solution and follow-up.

> *"Maybe we should find a different instrument to rehearse."*

Deal with problematic participants

There are times when you need to deal with problematic and difficult meeting participants. Keeping your meeting moving and active can eliminate many potential problems, but some participants may feel the need to monopolize the meeting, distract others, and refuse to participate. Here are some ways to work with them to get their behavior under control.

Encourage New People

Some attendees may hesitate to participate when the group could benefit from their comments. Try posing a question and asking how many people have comments about that topic. When new hands are raised, you can call on individuals to share their thoughts.

Is It That Bad?

Some individuals really know how to "push our buttons." We need to be careful about overreacting to moderately bad behavior. Does the behavior really qualify as troublesome? If the person is a nuisance, you should talk to them after the meeting to see what the problem really is.

It's Not Personal

Remember that in most instances, bad behavior is not directed at you personally. If you find it is personal, it needs to be handled in private and should involve an adult to support your actions.

Listen to Attendees

Meeting leaders need to listen, even when the person speaking won't be quiet. It is useful to interrupt them and summarize important parts. Specifically ask another person to speak or respond after thanking the person for his or her input.

Make Changes

If problems persist, change the way participation is handled. Break the group into pairs or smaller groups instead of a large group. The smaller groups also give the troublemakers a smaller audience so they can be reined in.

Nonverbal

Many times, the leader can make eye contact with the person causing a problem. Move closer to people who are talking to others during the meeting or who start to doze off.[19]

Rules

It might be necessary to create rules about group participation and communication. You can instruct attendees that their comments need to build on previous comments, and ask that they respect others' opinions. Each

---

19. Don't stare at them, though. That's creepy.

attendee should give his or her personal thoughts without trying to speak for others.

Get back on track

These are some common ways to settle conflicts and get the meeting back on track.

- Make the objectives clear to all attendees.

- Keep the group focused on the facts and any information that supports them.

- Stop the discussion for the time being.

- Sometimes some tactful and well-placed humor will do the trick, but be sure the person can handle humor.

- Find alternatives. Are there other ways to reach a decision? This would be a good time for Plan B.

- Be understanding. Take the time to listen, and work to understand what the other person is saying to you.

ROBERT'S RULES QUICK REFERENCE:
How to Withdraw a Motion

Why would I want to do this?

You want to take back a motion you brought up.

- After being called on, you can say, **"Madame/Mr. President, I move to withdraw my motion."**

When the group is stuck on a problem or you get the feeling you have hit a brick wall, switch gears briefly and give everyone a chance to regroup. Many times, that is all it takes to loosen everyone up and to get ideas flowing again. It's amazing how a little change can help your attendees think of new ways to approach a situation. Which of these ideas will work for your group?

- **Take a Slow, Deep Breath:** Ask all attendees to take ten slow, deep breaths. They should inhale deeply and exhale deeply. These are cleansing breaths, which can help refresh the body and mind.

- **Take a Break:** Sometimes you just need to give your attendees a short break. Let them get a drink, stretch their legs, and get out of the meeting room for a few minutes.[20]

- **Musical Chairs:** If the meeting goes stagnant, have attendees switch seats. This idea works even better when they move to a different part of the room. They can move from one side to the other and get a different perspective on the room and on the topics you are talking about.

- **Change the Topic:** When the group is really stuck, sideline a specific topic and move on to something completely different.

Find solutions

When the problems are discovered, it is critical to find solutions. Any issues need to be handled quickly and effectively. The longer problems drag on, the more people feel it is acceptable to cause problems, and the more they disrupt the meetings.

---

20. Remember to tell them to return to the meeting, though. It's counterproductive if meeting attendees think it's time to go home.

Fast Fact ——————————————————————

The Didgeridoo was developed by indigenous Australians and is still used today.

ROBERT'S RULES QUICK REFERENCE:
How to Postpone Definitely

Really, why would I want to do this?

You would choose to postpone definitely if you want the membership to have more time to consider the question.

- You can choose to move discussion to another time or day

- You can also choose to move discussion to come up for further consideration

Quick notes:

Can I interrupt the speaker? **No.** Second needed? **Yes.** Debatable? **Yes.** Amendable? **Yes.**

Vote needed? **Majority.**

CASE STUDY: AMIR WATYNSKI

President of Watt Media, Inc.
www.watt-media.com

Julie is President of her High School's Student Government, and has called a meeting for the Homecoming Committee to discuss this year's event, which is to take place in two months. The focus of the meeting will be the Homecoming Dance. Her committee consists of eight students — all who serve on the student government.

Julie starts the meeting by passing out the agenda, which includes finding and hiring a DJ, florist, deciding on food, and planning the Homecoming King and Queen crowning ceremony. As soon as everyone receives a copy, and as Julie is about to begin, Tim, the student programming vice president, blurts out, "We should use my uncle as a DJ, he is really great! I am also against having a Homecoming King and Queen. It's a bad tradition, it makes people compete, and I don't like it."

Trying to regain control of the meeting, Julie politely asks Tim to wait until those items are addressed. Tim reluctantly agrees, and allows Julie to continue. As the subject of hiring a DJ comes up, Tim again insists on hiring his uncle. He provides several reasons why the school should do so. Others disagree, stating that there are other DJs available and that they should be considered as well. Tim is defiant and stubborn.

As they move on and start discussing the Homecoming King and Queen, Tim again states his case strongly. He seems unwilling to compromise, and provides several reasons why this tradition should be stopped. Tim seems to make a strong case, with many details and support for his cause, but others question his motivations, and his opinions and perceptions seem skewed and unreasonable at times.

How should Julie deal with Tim?

Handling different personalities can surely be a challenge. There are so many personality types and many competing factors, including personal agendas.

First, Julie should try to empathize with Tim and see things from his point of view. Does he have a valid argument? Is his opinion driven by an opposing yet valid perspective, or is he operating from a hidden personal agenda?

If Julie determines that Tim's feelings are valid, she should acknowledge this, and, with a consensus from the entire committee, try to find a reasonable compromise. For example, Tim would like to have his uncle considered to be the DJ for the Homecoming Dance. Is it because Tim honestly believes his uncle is great at what he does and will bring a great energy to the party? If so, the committee would certainly be right to consider him.

If, however, Tim is driven by a selfish agenda to hire a family member, then Julie cannot allow the committee to proceed with that proposal. The same judgments should be applied to Tim's other request.

As president, Julie will often have to consider various ideas and points of view. In each case, she needs to weigh all sides and think about the consequences of her possible decisions.

If a compromise can be reached, she should always strive for a win-win solution. When this isn't possible, Julie needs to be firm and keep the common good in mind. This is one quality that can make her a strong leader.

Amir Watynski is the president of Watt Media, a leading web marketing firm in South Florida since 1998. He is also president of Temple Beth Torah Sha'aray Tzedek, a Jewish conservative synagogue with a membership of over 400 families. He served on the board of directors of the Chamber of Commerce of Coral Springs for six years. Amir runs all of the meetings in the temple and also conducts an annual membership meeting for all members. He lives in Coral Springs, Florida with his wife and two boys.

Games to Find Solutions to Problems

Here are a couple of games that your group can play to find solutions to problems within the group or with attendees.

Myers-Briggs Personality Test

The Myers–Briggs Type Indicator (MBTI) is a test designed to indicate psychological preferences in how people perceive the world and make decisions. It's based on the theory that humans experience four principal psychological functions: sensation, intuition, feeling, and thinking. Have members of your organization take the test and see which "type" fits their personality in order to see how they function in the group. You can find a version of the test at **www.16personalities.com/personality-types**.[21]

Myers-Briggs time wasters

Figured out your "type" yet? After you've taken the Myers-Briggs test, organize attendees into groups based on their personalities. Have them list the top 10 time wasters they can think of, and have them compare lists with the group. Which time wasters did they have in common? What are the biggest time wasters in your area? What suggestions do they have to limit the amount of time that is wasted? After you've tried this activity, mix up the Myers-Briggs types and ask them to repeat the game. Are there differences in answers?

Change is part of life

This activity helps the group learn that change is necessary and how it is easier to work with changes rather than fight them. Divide into groups of four or five people, and ask them to discuss the following questions:

- What was a recent change in the organization?

- Did people resist the change?

- Why? Why not?

- How could people have made the change easier?

21. Once you find out your personality type, visit **www.celebritytypes.com** to see your Myers-Briggs celebrity twin!

ROBERT'S RULES QUICK REFERENCE:
How to Clarify Parliamentary Rules

Why would I want to do this?

You are unsure of some of the parliamentary rules.

- Without being called on, you say, **"Point of parliamentary inquiry."**

CASE STUDY: PAIGE ARNOF-FENN
Founder & CEO of Mavens & Moguls
www.mavensandmoguls.com

Meetings can be an incredibly productive way to get a group together to make decisions, brainstorm ideas, or troubleshoot an existing project. They can also be a huge waste of time where there are multiple conversations going on simultaneously with no one guiding the discussion. So, how do you make the most of each meeting and ensure that the time together is well spent?

One trick I learned when I worked in Corporate America right after school was the rule that every meeting needed a PAL — **P**urpose, **A**genda and, time Limit to be successful. It turns out that if everyone invited to the meeting knows why he or she is there, what the agenda is, and how much time will be spent on each topic, your meeting will turn out great! This way, if people need to do some research in advance or have a pre-meeting to discuss something before bringing it up in front of the full group, they have time to prepare and no time is wasted around the table.

This process sends a very powerful message to the organization and affects the culture of the group, too. It communicates that your time is valuable and that we want you to perform at your best, contribute where you can, and always be prepared. It is a great feeling to solve problems and watch productivity grow. Nothing happens in a vacuum alone; it takes a lot of people (and meetings!) to move the needle, no matter what kind of club or organization you're a part of. There is a huge sense of pride and satisfaction when you're associated with a winning team.

Success is not luck or coincidence. It takes a lot of work and a lot of people working together toward a common goal. Meetings are a way to communicate and keep everything moving forward, so you might want to suggest bringing a PAL to your next one.

Paige Arnof-Fenn is the founder and CEO of the global marketing firm Mavens & Moguls, based in Cambridge, Massachusetts. Clients include Microsoft, Colgate, Virgin, Delta Airlines, non-profits, and venture-backed startups. Paige started her marketing career at companies such as Procter & Gamble and The Coca-Cola Company, so she has attended and led many meetings throughout her career. She also serves on and has chaired several boards, as well as being a popular speaker at industry events and conferences. A graduate of Stanford University and Harvard Business School, Paige has been a columnist at both Entrepreneur and Forbes.

11

Ending on a High Note

You've covered all your topics. Your agenda was on point. No one cried, threw chairs, or stormed out of the room. It's closing time — you're ready to get out of that stuffy meeting room and head home for dinner. But how do you actually end your meeting?

Believe it or not, ending a meeting isn't as simple as just shouting "It's done! Get out of here!" Having a strong ending is just as important as a strong opening, so you'll want to be mindful of the conclusion of your meeting.

CASE STUDY: MARK MCMILLION

Founder, McMillion Leadership Associates
www.mcmillionleadership.com

Everyone in the meeting needs to have a clear understanding of the next, most immediate action that needs to take place. While everyone may not be part of that action or task, he or she needs to realize what it is, who is going to do it, and when it must be done.

Let's talk about that in a little more detail. The task should be clearly laid out. For example, using the prom example from earlier, the next step (or one of the next steps) may be to contact DJs and bands for the music. The group should quickly identify the relevant information the people need. For the prom, this would probably be the date and duration, for instance, April 29, from 7-11 p.m. That's the information the person needs to go the DJs and bands so they can say whether they're available and how much they want to charge.

The next piece of the puzzle is what information needs to be gathered to make the decision. We talked about this in the problem-solving section a little bit. For this example, it may simply be a dollar amount. But there might be other information that could be useful as well such as recommendations (DJ Disco Duck did East High School's prom last year and really rocked it) and reputation (no one likes that band "The Space Chimps"; they just monkey around). The criteria the group wants to use to make the decision should be laid out so the person knows what to ask for and seek out. You may also want to specify a specific number of options.

Second, when do we need this? It might be by the next planning committee meeting or some other milestone. Remember: Even though you may decide in the meeting when you want to make a decision, there may be external factors as well. For instance, the band or DJ may have competing offers for the same day and want to decide sooner. Even though you may not know that up front, you still make a plan and then adjust as necessary.

Lastly, everyone needs to know, *very specifically*, who's doing what. "Mark, you're going to get us information on at least three DJs, and,

Michelle, you're going to find a few bands. Right?" By stating the task and the person's name, and then asking the question, you're making it clear who is doing what. Their response indicates they understand and lets everyone else know who's doing what.

You should do this as you go through the meeting, but as part of closing the meeting, a quick recap is appropriate. Chances are you've identified several tasks that need to be done, and it's a good idea to verify a second time that everyone is on the same page. This is also the opportunity to find out who has taken on too much and who hasn't stepped up at all.

In most groups, there are three types of people: Those gung-ho, enthusiastic ones who will take on anything and everything; those who will do what they are asked to do (but won't necessarily volunteer); and finally, those who want to be at the meeting but don't want to do anything. At the final roll-up, you may find that two or three people have taken on lots and lots of stuff, while everyone just took up oxygen. That's when the meeting owner needs to share the wealth (and work!) by balancing out the workload.

After this final roll call of tasks, it's also a good idea to *quickly* review the purpose of the meeting and then the *why* of the meeting. For instance, "Okay, we met today to figure who is handling the music and decorations for the prom. We did that (yay us!), and we're well on our way to having the best prom in the history of high school proms!"

Mark McMillion retired as a lieutenant colonel from the United States Army after 22 years on active duty. A graduate of West Point, he also earned a master's degree from The Ohio State University and taught at the Academy. During his time in the Army, he has literally attended and/or hosted over a thousand meetings. Unfortunately, only a handful were useful! The good news is those were the ones where he was in charge. You can get to know him better at www.mcmillionleadership.com, or follow him on Twitter @markmcmillion91.

Working Together to Reach a Consensus

Example: Let's say the Student Council is trying to decide the theme of the Homecoming dance. You've narrowed it down to the following options:

- "Alice in Zombieland"

- "Famous Historical Pets"

- "A Night in the U.S. House of Representatives"[22]

You and your group can't seem to decide on one of these themes, and you need to reach a consensus. To reach an educated agreement, the group needs to ask questions and discuss the idea in detail. It takes longer in the early stages, but it will save unnecessary reworking later. The group will discover more options, analyze more plausible ideas, and then find the best possible solution. When the group works together to find the best answer, everyone wins. The individuals feel good about their contribution. Members of your organization will feel that they contributed and all angles were evaluated before the final decision was reached.

How does your group reach a consensus about the homecoming dance? This might be one of the most mysterious facets of meeting procedures.[23] A consensus can only be reached through discussion. It is built in pieces as each idea is generated and evaluated by the group.

These are some of the characteristics of a group that will reach a consensus:

- All participants are involved. They understand that they can expect to contribute useful information to the process. Some ideas will be more raw than others, but the group will work together and add details to the ideas being considered.

- The points that your group agrees on need to be summarized by the leader or facilitator. Ideas that everyone agrees on should

---

22. I dare you to host a school dance using one of these themes.
23. Meeting procedures, by the way, are not particularly mysterious.

be noted along with areas of concern. Any concerns can be discussed further.

- The group should discuss positive and negative aspects of any idea. All members of your organization should be encouraged to state their concerns.

- When the group has an idea for a solution that contains potential problems, they need to be discussed in more detail.

ROBERT'S RULES QUICK REFERENCE: *How to Adjourn*

Really, why would I want to do this?

You would choose to adjourn if you would like the meeting to end.

- After being called on, of course, you can say, **"Madame/Mr. Chairman, I move to adjourn."**

Quick notes:

Can I interrupt the speaker? **No.** Second needed? **Yes.** Debatable? **No.** Amendable? **No.**

Vote needed? **Majority.**

It will be obvious when the group has a consensus. The concerns will be worked out, the solution along with a plan of action will take shape, and the group will agree on it. The facilitator or leader needs to recognize when the group reaches this point. When the group is near the point of reaching a consensus, the following questions can be asked to confirm where the group is in the process.

- "Where do we stand on the decision about the theme of the homecoming dance? Does anyone have additional concerns that we need to discuss?"

- "Is everybody in agreement? If not, what additional information do we need to cover?"

- "We can move to the next part of the agenda unless anyone has other questions."

- "Is there anything in this solution that we do not feel confident presenting to the student body?"

Remember: A consensus should not be a compromise. When people compromise, they give up key elements that are important to them. When a true consensus is reached, each person in the group feels comfortable with the final decision. No one should give up points he or she feels are important. For this to happen, each person in the group must speak honestly and freely with the other participants.

Helpful methods

Here are some techniques you can use to reach a consensus in your meetings, especially if you have more than two options to choose from.

- List all options on a flip chart. Combine similar options to create fewer choices.

- Let the participants take a few minutes to consider the list.

- Let participants cast a ballot for each option that sounds possible to them. They can vote for more than one but should not vote for all choices.

- Tally the ballots and discuss the remaining choices. At that point, vote again and eliminate more choices. Keep narrowing the list down until you make a final choice.

- If time is limited, let each attendee vote for one or two methods he or she likes best. The vote can be on paper or by a show of hands. Repeat until you narrow the list down to a manageable size. Once the list is shortened, the group should discuss the remaining choices in more detail.

Start small

It's much easier to reach a conclusion with a small group, which makes this method affective:

- Review the issue that is under discussion and address some of the ideas and thoughts that have been shared by the group.

- Ask participants for their thoughts about the review.

- Separate the group members into smaller groups.

- Each group needs to pick one person to present its proposal to the group.

- Each proposal should be listed on a flip chart or other board.

- The larger group can then discuss the ideas submitted by the small groups.

- The smaller groups go back to work on areas where there are debate.

- Once the debate is handled, the smaller group presents its proposal again.

Polling the group

Polling is a great way to gauge the group and see how far apart the attendees are in making a decision. This also indicates what points need to be discussed in more detail before there can be a resolution.

- Notify all participants that no more ideas will be presented or accepted on a particular topic.

- Review the plan and explain the steps to reach a consensus. Members of your group may accept the plan, decide the plan is fair, disagree with the plan, disagree with the decision, or express their concerns about the proposed plan.

- Make a list of the possible ideas on your flip chart. Each attendee needs to state his or her thoughts on these ideas. A simple headcount can work.

- When the results are tallied, announce them to the group. This shows you what ideas need to be discussed in more detail.

- Ask the attendees for their comments. Even if only one person has an issue with the idea, listen to that person.

Will any of these techniques help your group reach a consensus for the homecoming dance? Are there ways to make adjustments to these ideas to make them work for your group? Do you need to come up with new themes, or do you plan on going to the dance dressed as Bo, the Obama family dog? I like to take a variety of ideas and create methods that work for a specific group of people. You never know what idea will spark the best possibilities for your meeting.

ROBERT'S RULES QUICK REFERENCE: *How to Move the Previous Question*

What is this and why would I want to do it?

Previous question should be moved when you think discussion has dragged on for too long and you want members to vote.

- After you have been called on, you say, **"Madame/Mr. Chairman, I move the previous question."**

Quick notes:

Can I interrupt the speaker? **No.** Second needed? **Yes.** Debatable? **No.** Amendable? **No.**

Vote needed? **Two-thirds.**

Maintaining individuality within the group

When a group of people works together for a long time, they begin to have groupthink. As you've learned from earlier chapters, groupthink has its good and bad points. Members of your organization will work in sync, which is beneficial, but they may stop expressing their personal thoughts and just go along with the group, which cuts its effectiveness.

Another situation where this can happen is when the people making the decisions are too far removed from the day-to-day operations of the organization, such as your supervisor. In businesses, aka "real life," this can happen when a board of directors makes a decision without actual input from people who work on the project.

One other time when members suppress their thoughts is when the group wants to wrap the meeting up even though the problems may not be resolved and the decisions may not be made. The meeting could be running late, or there could be pressure to make a decision. When there is a lot of pressure, people may keep concerns to themselves to get a quicker resolution without taking the time to get the best solution.

These tips can help your group keep from falling into this trap:

- Create a diverse group with various experience and backgrounds.

- Group members need to have different points of view.

- The leader or facilitator needs to make attendees feel comfortable enough to share their thoughts about topics being discussed in your meeting.

- Decisions should be postponed until the group feels good about the resolution.

- Get the opinions of other people who have useful information to share.

- Listen to the input being offered in a positive manner.

Before the Meeting Ends

One huge attendee complaint is that meetings do not end on time. Try to stay within your time frame as often as possible. This helps the group maintain their commitment, enthusiasm, and positive attitude about your organization and its goals. When leaders let meetings run over their time limit, they indicate that they don't value their attendees' time.

ROBERT'S RULES QUICK REFERENCE:
How to Postpone Indefinitely

OK, why would I want to do this?

You would choose to postpone indefinitely if you want to kill a motion being discussed OR you are against a motion and want to learn what side other members are on.

- You would say, **"Madame/Mr. Moderator, I move to postpone the question indefinitely."**

What is a moderator?

The moderator is in charge of keeping the debate organized and timely

- You can also choose to say, **"Madame/Mr. Moderator, I move to postpone the motion indefinitely."**

Quick notes:

Can I interrupt the speaker? **No.** Second needed? **Yes.** Debatable? **No.** Amendable? **No.**

Vote needed? **Majority.**

People have mentioned that long meetings are a reason they do not volunteer for groups. In a business situation, employees may have no choice about attending meetings. There are two options—end the meeting on time, or discuss how much additional time is needed to find a solution with the participants.

No matter how much time you have set aside for your meeting, it's important that your group determines the following information before the end:

- **What needs to be done?**

  Be specific about what you need to do. The more specific instructions are, the less possibility of confusion. Some of these things could include additional research and information, finding or requesting additional funding, writing an idea, or actually starting the project.

- **When does it need to be done?**

You'll want to set a realistic timetable for your event. Within your time frame, there should be checkpoints or goals to be reached to keep the team motivated and indicate that progress is being made. Include information about how the timeline will be handled and monitored.

- **Who will be responsible?**

  Assign each part of the action plan to someone before ending the meeting. Attendees can be volunteers, or the meeting leader can handpick people if needed. Assignees need to agree to the terms for your project.

Have you ever been in a meeting and you had a great idea, but you were afraid to bring it up because you knew the task would be assigned to you? Me too. In a group, you should have some "idea" people, while other people can form and create a plan of action. A leader or facilitator can motivate his or her people by not trying to force an assignment on the wrong person. Give people the opportunity to volunteer first; then, assign projects if there aren't enough volunteers.

When Your Time Is Up but You're Not Done

What do you do if your one-hour meeting is supposed to be over in five minutes and you still don't have anything figured out? You always have the option to stop on time no matter what is happening, but that might not be the most effective way to end on time.

A better way to end the meeting on time is to monitor each segment of the meeting. You can list times beside each agenda item. Schedules can include starting or ending time to keep you on track. If one segment runs over, another needs to be cut. Be careful that some parts of the meeting are not cut too short. Your timing will improve when a conscious effort is made to start and end on time. Even if the meeting starts late, it should still end on time.

Ending meetings on time shows that the leader and facilitator are organized, prepared, and have respect for attendees.

Fast Fact

Better start reading: There are 20 chapters in "Robert's Rules of Order."

12

Looking Back on Your Meeting

The student council meeting about the homecoming dance has ended. You've chosen "Night at the U.S. House of Representatives" for a theme, and everyone feels comfortable with the decision. The meeting wasn't too long or too short, and there were several donut breaks throughout. The members of student council have left to go home, leaving you, the leader, alone in the classroom to reflect. You sit back, put your feet up on the desk, and begin to wonder . . .

Did my meeting accomplish its goal? And if so, how do I find out? Also, are there any donuts left?

Find Out How You Did

Evaluating effectiveness of your meetings is incredibly crucial to success. There are many ways you can evaluate a meeting, and we will review a number of them. Most feedback will come from the participants of your meeting. Some of these people will give you verbal feedback as they are racing out the door, but that might not be helpful. Instead, you can ask participants for their thoughts before they leave. Try these questions:

- Did you read the agenda before the meeting?

- Did you prepare any information to share at the meeting?

- Did you share useful ideas and thoughts with the group?

- Do you understand your responsibilities based on the results of the meeting?

- What can we do to make preparation easier for future meetings?

- What can and should be improved in upcoming meetings?

Verbal Feedback

An easy way to gather feedback is through hand gestures.

A thumb pointed up for a good meeting.

Thumb pointing to the side for a so-so meeting.

Thumb pointed down for a bad meeting.[24]

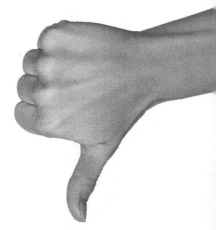

24. You can also have an option for "rock on," or when the index and pinky fingers are extended and parallel to each other.

At this point, you can have the participants write down their thoughts or share them with the group. Whatever you decide, it is important to hear from the people who offered a thumb turned down for a bad meeting. For more detailed and specific feedback, ask for an opinion of various portions of the meeting.

Some meetings end with each member sharing a couple of words about his or her favorite part. You could also ask about the least favorite parts of the meeting, or simply ask for attendee comments on the meeting.

The meeting facilitator may want to ask questions to get more details from the attendees. Some of these may include the following.

- What worked well in the meeting?

- What did not work well in the meeting?

- What could be improved?

- Are there any specific suggestions for ways to make improvements?

- How could the agenda be improved?

- How could more participation be generated?

The answers may be vague, but a good leader or facilitator can ask follow-up questions to get to the more specific information that is needed to make real improvements. Someone, such as your secretary, should be chosen to take names and record comments so that interviews can follow. It's helpful to end the feedback session with at least one clear way to make the next meeting better.

Written Feedback

There are some distinct advantages to gathering written feedback, including:

- People are usually more open and honest in writing than they are verbally and to your face.

- Some people express themselves better when they take a few minutes to form the words on paper.

- The written forms can be kept, and there is no chance of making incorrect notes as happens during a lively conversation.

- More information can be gathered on a form.

- The form can be tailored to your group to gather the information you need.

These forms are relatively simple to compile and should be easy to complete. Multiple choice is a favorite, because it is easy to answer. There are many types of scales that can be used, such as:

- Good, fair, bad

- 1 – 5, 1 being bad and 5 being good

- The Likert scale—strongly agree, agree, disagree, and strongly disagree

- Always, almost always, sometimes, rarely, and never

When you create questions to gather feedback, there are basic things you need to learn. Below is a selection of questions. Choose the ones that will work best for your group. You might want to change the questions from time to time instead of using the same questions at every meeting.

- Was the agenda sent early enough for adequate preparation?

- Did everyone arrive on time?

  If not, what could be changed to help people arrive on time?

- Did attendees get sufficient notice about the meeting?

- Was the agenda organized and suitable for the meeting goals?

- Should I drop out of school and join the circus?

- Did the meeting start on time?

- Was the goal of the meeting made clear from the beginning?

- Was only one topic discussed at a time?

- Did everyone in the meeting participate?

- Was their participation on topic and useful?

- Did more than one person talk at a time?

- Did my hair look stupid during the meeting?

- What could be done to ensure that only one person has the floor at a time?

- Did attendees feel they could speak their mind?

- Do the attendees show respect for each other and the meeting process?

- Did you like last week's episode of "The Bachelor"?

- Were questions used in the right way and to further understanding of the topic?

  If not, how could this be improved?

- Were points summarized after each section of the meeting?

- Were the discussions applicable to the topics on the agenda?

- Did the group review the positive and negative aspects of all topics?

- Were they discussed well?

- Were decisions made fairly and only after adequate discussion?

- Did the meeting progress at a reasonable pace?

- Should I bring a celebrity guest next time?

- Was the entire agenda discussed, or were parts skipped to end on time?

- Did the meeting reach the goals that were set out in the beginning?

- If not, what could be done to ensure this was accomplished at the next meeting?

- Were all action plans and assignments made clear for the attendees?

- Were the assignments fair and equal?

- Were plans for the next meeting mentioned?

- What was the overall atmosphere of the meeting?

- Did the meeting end on time?

- Should I bring more donuts in the future?

These are just some of the things you might want to ask. Remember, questions should be tailored to fit the problems that pertain to your group.

Once you ask pointed questions, you can also shift to more open-ended questions. After you have the specific information you want, you may want to ask: Are there any other comments, observations, or recommendations before we end the discussion? You do need input and feedback, but don't let the discussion go on too long. In instances where you have ongoing problems, it could be best to schedule a session just to discuss problems in the meetings and how to fix them. This can save a lot of frustrations and headaches at future meetings.

Online Feedback

Since we live in the digital age, it might be more convenient to receive feedback using online surveys and questionnaires. These are helpful because they sort the information in an easy-to-read way and are often faster than a typical written survey.

SurveyMonkey®

SurveyMonkey provides free, customizable surveys that you can email out to your organization. It is used by big-scale corporations, such as Facebook, but is also convenient for the average user. Visit **www.surveymonkey.com** for more information.

TrainingCheck

Another handy tool you can find online is TrainingCheck. This website allows you to evaluate workshops, training sessions, conferences, and meetings. You can customize your own questions, choose how to send the survey, and even decide how to configure the data after it's collected. Check out TrainingCheck at **www.trainingcheck.com**.

QuizWorks

The Online Quiz Creator by QuizWorks is geared towards publishers, teachers, and brands, but it can also be handy for meetings or just having fun. Offering both customizable surveys and already made surveys that are just for fun, the free version of this website has 15 questions per survey, allows 100 games per month, and five kinds of question types. Find the Online Quiz Creator at **www.onlinequizcreator.com**.

Final Notes

When you look back on your meeting, I hope you view it as a positive experience and use the feedback you've received to make your next meeting even better. While they can be incredibly boring, meetings should be a positive experience that allow you to accomplish goals, solve problems, and develop professionally.

Also, they're a great way to get free food.

Conclusion

It's true. You've reached the end of this book.

In the beginning of our little adventure, I asked you to imagine a meeting. If you imagined a nightmarish, painful, or just plain dull meeting, I hope you've changed your mind. While a meeting can definitely be a negative experience, you now have the tools to make them fun, educational, and productive. And that, my friends, is a life-long skill.

We talked about different types of meetings and how to evaluate whether you need a meeting. We had a chapter on how to choose the right location for your meeting, when to schedule it, and whom to invite. You learned how meeting tools and equipment can affect your meeting, as well as the importance of finding solutions and keeping members of your organization on track.

Each of these subjects may not seem very important to some people, but combine all the elements that were discussed, and you have a recipe for a successful and effective meeting. Also, as a final note, remember that the suggestions and information in this book are just guidelines for you to use when creating and planning the most effective meetings possible. The actual strategies you should use will be determined by your leadership style and the individual needs of your organization. Good luck on holding meetings, and remember—always bring donuts!

Appendix A: Sample Agenda

Sample Agenda

Group Name: Student Council
Meeting Title: Donut Budget
Meeting Organizer: Hannah

Date: April 2
Start Time: 4:20 p.m.
Ending Time 5:20 p.m.

Materials Needed for Meeting: Donuts, pencils, a butterfly net
What Should Participants Bring: Notes, a smile, running shoes

Goals for the Meeting: Decide the budget for the Donut Scavenger Hunt, eat food, solve the mystery of the Roanoke Colony Disappearance.[25]

Meeting Leader: Hannah
Facilitator: Larry

Recorder: Gretchen
Decision Maker: The Group

Group Members to be Included: Bill Ding, Dina Soares, Hazel Nuttee, Dave "The Big Squeeze" Johnson, Anna Conda
Special Notes for Attendees or Leader: Bring more donuts next time (preferably the chocolate kind)

---

25. A historical event where members of the colonial Roanoke colony disappeared in Virginia in 1590 without a trace.

Appendix B: Sample Constitution

I. Name of the Organization

Section 1: The official name of this organization is the Donut Enthusiast Club of James River High School in Atlanta, Georgia.

II. Purpose or Mission Statement

Section 1: The purpose of this organization is to teach members about the history of donuts and the donut industry; how to make donuts themselves and how to use food to create a more hospitable, inviting atmosphere at school, home, and work; the importance of a balanced diet alongside moderate consumption of sweets; to give students experience in a professional setting; and to provide resources for those wanting to enter the food service industry.

Section 2: The Donut Enthusiast Club will abide by all of the rules for clubs created by the administration of James River High School.

III. Qualifications for Membership in the Organization

Section 1: All members must be full-time students of James River High School. Freshmen, sophomores, juniors, and seniors are all equally qualified for membership.

Section 2: Members pay an annual $25 membership fee and must maintain a 2.5 GPA. If a member's GPA falls below 2.5, he or she will be placed on a semester's probation. He or she is still permitted to participate in and vote in all the meetings and is not barred from attending the events; however, he or she is required to meet with our academic services mentor once a month for free tutoring, study resources, and more. If his or her GPA is still lower than a 2.5 after one semester—except in cases of serious illness, either his or her own or a close family member's; the death of a family member; and other significant family disturbances—he or she will be removed from membership. If his or her circumstances match the exceptions, he or she will be on probation for as many semesters as the situation occurs without being removed from membership.

Section 3: There are three types of members in the organization:

1. **Active Members:** Active members are current freshmen, sophomores, juniors, and seniors who are in accordance with the rules of the organization. They attend all mandatory meetings, pay their membership dues, and regularly participate in events.

2. **Inactive Members:** Inactive members are not in accordance with the rules of the organization, whether they have not paid their dues by the deadline (two weeks after the matriculation ceremony) or do not attend the requisite number of meetings for a semester. They are allowed to attend all events and all meetings, but they cannot vote.

3. **Alumni Members:** Alumni members are graduates of James River High School who were in the Donut Enthusiast Club for all or part of their time here or students who moved to another school but were members of the Donut Enthusiast Club for at least a semester. Alumni are welcome to attend meetings and events.

Section 4: The procedure of matriculating new members is the following: The Donut Enthusiast Club begins meeting on the Monday when classes start for a new school year. All current members pledge to put posters in appropriate spots around the school, talk to their fellow students about the school, and hold two mixers for new members (in addition to regularly scheduled events for the Donut Enthusiast Club) within the first two weeks of class. Applications are distributed at the mixers, and information about how to get an application must be on all of the posters (the secretary will always be in charge of emailing out applications to prospective members). Within three weeks of school starting, applications will be due. Within four weeks of school starting, applications will be reviewed, and there will be a matriculation ceremony within five weeks of school starting (again, in addition to regularly scheduled events).

The same procedure will be followed at the beginning of the second semester. This means that there are two opportunities per school year to receive new members.

The application form will consist of the following: the student's name, birthdate, address, phone number, year in school, and GPA (if second-semester freshman or higher; otherwise, first-semester freshman can leave this spot blank); the telephone number and email address of a former teacher who would be willing to attest to the student's academic qualifications and desire for extracurricular enrichment and experiences; and a 250-word statement on why he or she wants to join the club. (Students with lower than a 2.5 GPA can be admitted on probation.)

IV. Rules of the Organization

Section 1: The Donut Enthusiast Club has a meeting every Monday at 4:00 p.m. during the school year. Two-thirds of members must be present to create a quorum. Members must be present for two-thirds of the meetings each semester to be active members, with exceptions for very bad weather, family emergencies, serious illness, family member's death, and other serious disturbances. Members who cannot attend should inform the secretary of the organization in as much advance as possible.

Section 2: There are no rules or punishments about attending events since they occur at varied times that students cannot block out into their schedules. The Donut Enthusiast Club will have at least two public events per semester that are open to the entire school (including students, faculty, and staff) and/or parents and siblings. (The members of the club can choose the audience based upon the nature of the event.) They will also have at least two private events per semester at the school for the members of the Donut Enthusiast Club and/or their families. Furthermore, at least once a semester, the club will have an event outside the school, whether attending a donut shop, a workshop on entrepreneurship, and other opportunities. If a member seldom attends events, the president of the organization will meet with him or her to discuss the situation and find a good solution. (For instance, maybe the events always seem to conflict with the student's part-time job.)

V. Meeting Rules

Section 1: All meetings will be governed by parliamentary procedure. Each member is expected to read "Robert's Rules of Order" (the most recent edition) and ask the parliamentarian about any questions. A copy will be provided to every new member at the matriculation ceremony.

Section 2: All meetings will be approximately one hour long, and there will always be a donut break at 4:30 p.m. The business of the meeting will stop for five minutes, and members can continue to eat donuts when the meeting recommences. The president will be in charge of bringing donuts.

VI. Qualifications of and Duties of Officers

Section 1: Members can only participate in each position once for one school year. I.e.: a person can be secretary only once, but being secretary does not disqualify him or her from running for another role.

Section 2: Secretary: The secretary is elected for a term lasting a school year. He or she takes notes at every meeting (if he or she is unable to attend, the treasurer takes notes), takes care of all email correspondence, and is in charge of administrative tasks generally.

Treasurer: The treasurer is elected for a term lasting a school year. He or she receives all membership dues and keeps a meticulously tidy Excel spreadsheet of the organization's finances.

President: The president is elected for a term lasting a school year. He or she sets the agenda for all the meetings and facilitates all events.

Vice President: The vice president is elected for a term lasting a school year. He or she directs the meetings in the president's absence and assists the presidents with meetings and events.

Academic Services Mentor: The academic services mentor is elected for a term lasting a school year. He or she is always willing to meet with members to suggest academic resources.

Parliamentarian: The parliamentarian is elected for a term lasting a school year. He or she is the arbiter of whether or not parliamentary procedure is being followed correctly at meetings.

Section 3: Two of the following four leaders must be present at every meeting: secretary, treasurer, president, and vice president.

VII. Election Process

Section 1: Elections are held two weeks following the matriculation ceremony. At the meeting before elections (which are held during the regular Monday meeting), all candidates submit a form explaining the position(s) they are running for and why they want to do so. Members in good standing who have been part of the club for one semester or more are eligible. At the regularly scheduled meeting the subsequent Monday, which will last more than an hour but no more than three hours, each candidate will give a speech, the length of which is determined by the number of candidates.

Section 2: Running for more than two positions is prohibited. If a candidate wins two positions, he or she picks the position he wants more, and the other position goes to the person with the second highest number of votes.

Section 3: The candidate who gets a majority of votes wins the position. If there is a tie, the sitting president, who does not vote, casts the deciding vote.

Section 4: If a leader has to leave the school mid-semester or at the end of a semester, a special election will be held simply to fill that position. Members not currently in position of leadership are the only ones eligible. If the replacement leader will only be the in the position for part of a semester, it does not count toward the yearlong restriction; if he or she will be in the position for more than a semester (for instance, if a member has to leave the school in mid-October, and he or she had just been elected to a position that would last until the school year ended in June), the yearlong restriction does apply to the new leader.

Glossary

Acceptance – signing a contract

Acknowledgement – written notice of confirmation for a guest

Actual Budget – current, real budget

Advance Deposit – money paid in advance to secure room or refreshments

Advance Registration – potential attendees can register before the event

Ad Hominem – an argument directed against a person rather than the position he or she is maintaining

Agenda – outline, list, or plan to be followed for the meeting

Arbitration – procedure used to resolve problems or dispute without going to court

Attendee Data – demographic information about each attendee

Audio Conferencing – a live meeting on the phone

Authorized Signature – signature of person who can make and approve decisions

Auxiliary Business – outside business that is involved in a meeting

Auxiliary Service – outside services that are needed for the meeting

Badge – a tag used to identify attendees

Banquet – a fancy meal served to a number of people; can be to recognize someone

Banquet Event Order – a form used to list all details about a banquet

Bay of Pigs – a failed military invasion of Cuba in 1961

Board of Directors Style – double-width table used for conferences

Book – schedule an event in advance

Breakout Sessions – meeting participants are divided into small groups to work together on specific tasks for the group

Business Casual – a less formal style of dress instead of a suit and tie or dress

Cancellation Clause – a contract clause that outlines the damages if the contract is terminated

Classroom Style – seats are arranged in rows and face the conductor; all attendees have a place to take notes

Clause – portion of a contract that pertains to a specific subject

Complete Meeting Package – a plan that includes all meals, lodging, and services

Complimentary Room – meeting room which is furnished at no charge

Conference Style – seats are arranged around all sides of the tables

Confirmation – reservations are verified

Confirmation Letter – written verification of a reservation

Conflict of Interest – document that requires speaker to reveal any conflicts with your organization

Contract – legally binding agreement between parties

Devil's Advocate – a person who expresses a different opinion to test the strength of opposing views

Demographic Profile – group statistical information about participants (age, location, gender, income, and other details)

Dress Code – type and style of clothing that is acceptable

Duty Roster – hourly schedule that outlines all staff member duties

Facilitator – person expected to keep the meeting on track

Floor Plan – drawing to scale that shows the room arrangement

Function – planned meeting

Function Sheet – details relating to planned meeting

Function Space – area that is reserved for meeting

Groupthink – tendency of a group to think alike

Head Count – number of people in attendance

Host – person who will assist speaker before, during, and after meeting

Incidentals – minor expenses that are not detailed

Invitation Letter – letter sent to a potential speaker asking them to attend your meeting

Keynote – opening statement or remarks

Keynote Speaker – person who gives the primary speech

Lectern – a stand that is elevated to hold reading materials, notes, or visual aids

Meeting History – information and details about past meetings

Meeting Profile – report with details about former meetings

Mediator – a person who attempts to make people involved in a conflict come to an agreement

Moderator – person who oversees the meeting

Networking – a chance to exchange information between people and businesses

No-Show Report – a report that details the attendees who do not show up and did not cancel

Off-Site Event – meetings held somewhere other than your school or regular meeting place

Outside Vendor – vendor who provides services for meeting or event

Outsourcing – bringing in people from the outside to work on a meeting or event

Overbooking – scheduling multiple events or meetings on a specific day, time, and location

Program Development – planning before an event to determine content and format

Point of Order – a parliamentary procedure tactic used when someone is disobeying the rules of the meeting

Point of Privilege – a parliamentary procedure tactic used to ask others to speak up

Point of Information – a parliamentary procedure tactic used to ask the speaker a question

Quorum – the minimum number of members at a meeting that would make the proceedings of that meeting valid

Reasonable Accommodation – facilities must make reasonable efforts to accommodate people with disabilities or hardships

Registrant – meeting attendee who is registered beforehand

Report – details used to evaluate meeting

Room Capacity – total number of people who can be in a room comfortably

Skirting – fabric placed around the bottom of tables for a meeting or event

Staging Guide – a notebook that contains room layouts, function sheets, and any other information needed for meetings or events

Table Top Display – visual aids that are placed on top of a table

Teleconferencing – people from different regions that meet without leaving their locations; the live feed enables the participants to interact with each other

Video Conference – a digital meeting that allows people to meet face-to-face with no regard to their physical location; the conference can include visual clips, graphics, and data or document transmissions

Webcasting – words, pictures, audio, and visual elements are delivered over the Internet

Bibliography

Dennis, Austin. "Artifact Details." Beginnings of PowerPoint: A Personal Technical Story. 2009. Web. 03 Aug. 2016. **www.computerhistory.org**.

Capretto, Lisa. "The Village People Talk About the Origin of Disco Classic 'Y.M.C.A.' (Video)." *The Huffington Post*. TheHuffingtonPost.com, 11 Feb. 2014. Web. 20 July 2016. **www.huffingtonpost.com**.

"Cmm." *Cmm*. 2016. Web. 05 July 2016. **http://oregonstate.edu**.

Cope, Jonathan. *How to Play the Didgeridoo: A Practical Guide for Everyone*. Great Britain: Wild Wind, 2000. Print.

Dockweiler, Steve. "How Much Time Do We Spend in Meetings? (Hint: It's Scary)." Themuse, 15 Oct. 2014. Web. 05 July 2016. **www .themuse.com**.

"Facebook Fast Facts." *CNN*. Cable News Network, 2016. Web. 05 July 2016. **www.cnn.com**.

Fields, Julian. "Speaking Without Words: Body Language and Non-Verbal Cues in Communication." *Lifesize*. 23 June 2015. Web. 20 July 2016. **www.lifesize.com**.

"Groupthink." *Communication Studies*. 26 May 2011. Web. 05 July 2016. **www.communicationstudies.com**.

"Guidelines." *Robert's Rules of Order*. Web. 05 July 2016. **www.roberts rules.org**.

Jennings, C. Allen. "Robert's Rules for Defining a Quorum." *Dummies. com*. For Dummies. Web. 20 July 2016. **www.dummies.com**.

Jurassic Parliament, 2016. Web. 8 Sept. 2016. **www.jurassicparliament .com**.

"LaMar's Fun Facts." *LaMars Donuts*. Web. 05 July 2016. **www.lamars.com**.

Laya, Patricia. "Study: What Makes a Team Smarter? More Women." *Business Insider*. Business Insider, Inc, 30 June 2011. Web. 20 July 2016. **www.businessinsider.com**.

Levenstein, Justin. "Email Statistics Report." *The Radicati Group* (2013): 2013. Web. 05 July 2016. **www.radicati.com**.

Lingle, Ruby. "Parliamentary Procedures: Interesting Facts and Tips." *Meeting Management*. 2005. Web. 05 July 2016. **http://extension.illinois .edu**.

Love, Jillian D'Onfro and Dylan. "11 Crazy-Interesting Facts About Google." *Business Insider*. Business Insider, Inc, 12 Aug. 2014. Web. 05 July 2016. **www.businessinsider.com.**

Mendez, Barbara. "The 7 Best Foods to Eat Before an Important Meeting." *Inc.com*. Web. 20 July 2016. **www.inc.com**.

Randerson, James. "Yawning Is Catching in Chimps." *New Scientist*. New Scientist, 21 July 2004. Web. 20 July 2016. **www.newscientist.com**.

Robert, Henry M. Robert's Rules of Order. Chicago: S. C. Griggs & Company. 1876.

Russell, Daniel. "An Analysis of Meeting Length." Attentiv, 20 Apr. 2015. Web. 05 July 2016. **http://attentiv.com**.

Wexler, Mark. "Expanding the Groupthink Explanation - International Cultic Studies Association (ICSA)." Cultic Studies Journal, 1995. Web. 05 July 2016. **www.icsahome.com**.

Index

About the Author

Hannah Litwiller is a freelance writer and cat astrologist. She has published articles in the *Truman Today* and *Truman Review*, as well as blog posts for The Olive Link and Truman Media Network. She has also been published in *Windfall* magazine. Hannah received her B.A. in public communication from Truman State University and currently resides in Kansas City. Her favorite F.R.I.E.N.D. is Phoebe Buffay. Follow Hannah on Twitter at @hlitwill.